A
SHORT HISTORY
OF
ENGLISH
CHURCH MUSIC

ERIK ROUTLEY

MOWBRAYS
LONDON & OXFORD

ISBN 0 264 66125 7

Printed in Great Britain by
Lowe & Brydone Printers Limited, Thetford, Norfolk

CONTENTS

Preface   v

1. Emerging from Infancy, *c*. 1100–1532   1

2. A Crisis of Cultures, 1532–1649   13

3. The New Professionals, 1649–1738   28

4. The Evangelical Age, 1738–1847   41

5. The New Seriousness, 1833–76   55

6. The Church Triumphant and Trivial,
   1851–99   64

7. The Creative Underground, 1848–1904   77

8. The Age of Confidence, 1900–55   89

9. Anxiety and Opportunity, 1955–75   104

Index   119

Dedicated with gratitude for abundant friendship and encouragement over a period now extending to more than a quarter of a century to

GERALD H. KNIGHT

Second Director (1953–72) of the Royal School of Church Music, Doctor of Music, and apostle of Church Music, of whom it can fittingly be said 'The world is his parish'

PREFACE

Anyone felicitous enough to be concerned with the location of specific buildings in a city, or with its drainage system, will reach for a map of that city which represents a mile by fifty inches. Anyone who plans a ten-mile walk will take a map on a 2½ inch scale. The traveller who wants to drive from London to Newcastle upon Tyne in half a day will take one that uses a ten-inch-to-the-mile scale. This book is like that—a quick journey, with a broad picture of the country but resisting the temptation to stop and dally in the picturesque places. Recently I have encountered those maddening American road maps which lead you to expect a T-junction when in fact there is an X-junction because they have decided to omit the fourth arm of the crossroads. Somehow I must try to see that this doesn't happen to my traveller too often, but there will not be room here to mark every disused windmill and every closed railway station.

Those who want larger-scale maps can readily find them. A very handy large-scale atlas, as it were, is Kenneth Long's massive book, *English Church Music* (Hodder & Stoughton, 1971). The series called *Studies in Church Music,* published between 1964 and 1973 by Barrie & Jenkins, provides more detailed information and criticism. E. H. Fellowes's classic, *English Cathedral Music* (Methuen, 1941, revised 1969 by J. A. Westrup: and you want both ideally because Westrup didn't see things the way Fellowes saw them) is a more specialized book; C. H. Philips's *The Singing Church* (Faber 1945, revised and reissued 1966) is somewhere between Kenneth Long and this one, and entirely commendable. For a more practical guide, there is *Church Music at the Crossroads,* by Lionel Dakers (Marshall, Morgan & Scott, 1970), very much in the down-to-earth tradition of Sydney Nicholson.

With all that available, it occurred to somebody that there was room for this one, and its scope, as suggested to me by those who asked me to write it, is adroitly adjusted to my own limitations. It is for those who are intelligently interested in English church music and in people, and who may or may not go on from here to acquire the more detailed and learned studies mentioned above.

Since obviously a book of this length can contain few music examples, I am bound to present a less complete picture than I should have liked, or than a reader might wish for. To make references as easy as possible I have confined specific references to material that can be found in the *Treasury of English Church Music* (five volumes published by Blandford Press, 1965 and edited by Gerald Knight and William Reed), the *Church Anthem Book* (Oxford, 1936) and the *Oxford Easy Anthem Book* (Oxford, un-dated, middle 1950s). Anything else I may refer to may illustrate what I say but the reader will not be crippled if he does not have it by him.

One other word, using our travelling metaphor once more, is to quote that folk tale which illustrates the more lovable aspects of Ireland, and which relates of how a traveller asked a native the way to (we will say) Ballybunion, and received the reply, 'If I wanted to go there I wouldn't start from here'. The reader is warned that, quite probably, the church music he knows best appears fairly late in the book, while the story has to begin with what perhaps he finds wholly unfamiliar: fourteenth century polyphony is still more often heard in the classroom than in the cathedral, let alone the parish church. I hope he will not be troubled by that, and I shall try to be more explanatory in the earlier pages than I shall need to be in the later.

1. EMERGING FROM INFANCY, *c.* 1100–1532

In one sense there must have been English church music as soon as Christians began singing in England—and that means before 200 A.D., when the place was called Britain, and was a remote outpost of the Roman Empire. But our story cannot begin there. Any Christians who were at worship before the time of Archbishop Augustine of Canterbury (597 A.D.) must have sung such songs as they had learnt in the Christian parts of Europe, or been taught by those who had so learned them. During the century that followed Augustine's mission, what could by then be called the English church was organized on a diocesan pattern; it became, as it were, a regional church rather than a mission outpost. We may suppose that thereafter its liturgies began to settle down on the lines followed by the older communities of Europe, and that something like a singing tradition established itself. But we cannot really know—and there is not much to be gained by trying to find out—how much of the music they sang was indigenous and how much imported. In any case the earliest liturgical manuscripts containing the system of office hymns in use at such places as Sarum (Salisbury) and York cannot be dated before 1000 A.D.

We are bound to begin with the first manuscripts available of medieval church music, which have fairly recently been transcribed by devoted scholars. Material from these is to be found in *Musica Britannica,* the earlier volumes, and more accessibly in volume I of the *Treasury of English Church Music.* But in order to understand the background of this music we must recall just what, in such days as those, people thought the business of the Church was. The best way to understand this is to read Bernard Manning's *The People's Faith in the Time of Wyclif,* or the opening chapter of the same author's *The Making of Modern English Religion.** Or, of course, *Piers Plowman* or *The Canterbury Tales.* From such sources as these one becomes aware of a culture separated from ours not merely by six or seven centuries but by a chasm which only a large effort of the imagination on the part of twentieth-century people can bridge. In the last words of the

---

* The first unhappily out of print; the second reissued 1967 by Tavistock Press.

former book mentioned above, Manning wrote: 'The medieval church is the mother of us all.' True; but we don't live at home any more.

We have to imagine a Europe in which the Church is the largest single organization, the largest employer of labour, the repository of all learning, and the arbiter of all thought. And it really was The Church, not The Churches, or a Council of Churches. It will not really be sufficient to think of the post-Tridentine Catholic Church (that is, that Church between 1570 and 1964) as any guide to what life 'was like in the medieval church. The Church really did brood over the Middle Ages. That did not mean that those ages were, in our modern sense, notably 'religious'. People were not then more moral, more spiritually minded, more compassionate, than they are now; certainly they were not more patient or more peaceable. But the Church was an axiom—something whose existence nobody questioned or thought in need of justification, even if they criticized it in detail. It nursed not only the theologians, but the scholars, the men of letters and the diplomats. It had a positive monopoly of literacy. If anything had to be written, the *clerks* (clerics) wrote it. And to a considerable extent ordinary people were similarly content to believe that the Church was responsible for praying and worshipping. They could put their prayers out to be done by the clerics much as nowadays we put out work which we are not ourselves qualified to do—such as performing surgery, attending to the plumbing or organizing' expeditions to the moon.

The Church then was in very big business indeed, and its worship was a highly professional vocation. This is where church music belonged. What church music of the Middle Ages survives is clearly professional music. One need not mean by that that it was beautifully performed, or even necessarily that is is written with unfailing skill (it is always possible to be over-romantic about distant things); but it was not music for a congregation at worship to have any part in. It may have been set to sacred words, it may have been set to metrical words, it may indeed have carried words which are known to us as the Latin texts behind certain familiar hymns; but it was music for people set aside to be musicians (or at least singers) to perform. This explains why it looks, to anyone who is not familiar with it, so outlandish and sometimes sounds so peculiar. But something else, of supreme aesthetic importance, explains it more cogently than this.

We are, with this early English church music, beginning in the twelfth century or so, coming into the story of music at a critical moment. We are overhearing what happens when something which has probably been in existence for a long time becomes, as it were, officially recognized: this is nothing less than the singing of more than one sound at a time.

Officially anyhow, music in the first thousand years of the church's life was monodic. It was plainsong. It was unaccompanied melody—and what melody it was, indeed! It is hardly surprising that, having, as it were, only one direction to travel in, it went a long way.

But this is where at once we encounter a principle which in any historical investigation of these things is of the greatest importance. Briefly the principle is, 'don't imagine that everybody in those days sang like the choir you have on record at home or performing in the nearest cathedral'. In this case—don't imagine that this plainsong always sounded like Solesmes. Who can imagine that every Christian community, sacred or secular, was composed of people who all sang comfortably at the same pitch? Any singing community in those days was either all men or all women: but this means in one group, basses and tenors, in the other, sopranos and altos, with the voice-range God gave them, True, it would be possible for a decently-endowed precentor so to pitch a simple plainsong chant that everybody present was able to sing it without distress. (The tone-deaf would, in a well-organized monastery, be peeling potatoes in the kitchen, at least once potatoes had been introduced to England). But take any more developed plainsong melody—even so relatively undemanding a piece as *Victimae Paschali* (EH 130), or, for a rather more complex and expressive one, the antiphon to *Pange Lingua* (EH 737), let alone the elaborate tropes and Alleluias which were heard at Mass on festive days: such a tune soon goes out of somebody's range—too high for low voices, or too low for high ones, unless they are well trained. Anybody knows what will happen. Somebody will be singing a fifth below, or maybe a fourth (or the same, above). Some not very good ears may be thinking that this is actually the right note to sing. Certainly, if ever people outside the liturgy joined in communal singing this will have happened. Naturally, the score being monodic provided for nothing of the sort; but from what we know of the development of polyphony it is just as if somebody said, 'well, what's *wrong* with this?' As soon as that question is answered liberally, we get a musical style official enough to be given a Latin name—*organum,* which primitively meant the doubling at the fourth or fifth of a melody, and later comes to mean the singing of a counter-melody.

But if anybody said, 'nothing's *wrong* with that', they fell before long into an aesthetic trap. Most of the time it sounds perfectly tolerable, but the scale to which their ears were (and ours are) tuned will sooner or later bring them to a point where the fifth is diminished or the fourth augmented. As an experiment, if a piano is handy, try playing the tune of *Conditor alme siderum* (EH 1) with a bass *organum* at the fifth. In the written key, or mode, there is no D flat. But at the seventh note you will need either a D flat, which is not in the mode, or a D, which produces with the upper A flat the sound that was always known as the *diabolos*, 'the devil's noise'. (Play the whole thing in C major using only white notes and the problem is even easier to isolate.) Nobody thought that a pleasing sound, and devices were at once invented to avoid it. The earliest of these was to give the secondary voice a range of five notes, and forbid it to go outside that range—a little like the rules of the board games people play at home. 'You must stay on your tonic, the same as our tonic, until we are far enough away from you to make a fourth or a fifth: then you can move with us—but you must not go outside your range.'* The result is, obviously, two different melodies (the second perhaps not a very enterprising one)—and there is the origin of polyphony.

Another way of avoiding the *diabolus* is to introduce the needed note that is not in the chosen scale—to flatten the B if the scale is that which uses our white notes—and there comes the polyphonic use of chromaticism. They called it 'mode-breaking': we call it introducing accidentals, but in medieval music for a long time the tradition was that only one note, the B, might be so modified.

Now once these two devices had established themselves and weathered the storms of indignation and doom which no doubt

* See the examples and text on pp. 253–5 of Gustav Reese, *Music in the Middle Ages*, which explain all this more amply and learnedly.

came from conservatives who must have been sure that this was introducing every possible sort of licentiousness into church music, what happened to music can be described only as its coming of age. From then onwards music was the one force which the authority of the Church could never subdue. One thing led to another, as the dogmatic doomwatchers predicted it would,* and by 1325 it became necessary for Pope John XXII to issue a directive indicating the bounds beyond which church composers ought not to go. It had no effect. Protest of this sort is Canute-like. Nothing could stop the tide of music once it had begun to run. The story of English church music, once this discovery of polyphony had taken place, is a steady crescendo of complexity, ingenuity and ecstasy.

It is fair to say that between 1400 and 1600 English church music was the most adventurous and vital music available to the whole Church. That period seems to be split in two by the Reformation—and we shall have to treat it so here; but in fact there is no failure in quality, no slump in invention or inspiration, from Dunstable to Gibbons. Indeed, the music is not only fine music but it is *English* music. Now historians easily show that the English church in the later Middle Ages was regarded by the sacred bureaucracy of Rome as a somewhat eccentric and unpredictable branch of their empire. You can put it that we were far enough from Rome to get away with more than people nearer the metropolis were allowed; or you can say, as I for one prefer to, that ever since the English were interdicted by Leo I for keeping Easter on the wrong day in A.D. 454 (to which they replied that the last news they had, in A.D. 314 was that Easter was on the day they were observing: to which Rome replied that the metropolitan mind had changed at least twice since then), or even ever since the Welsh Pelagius entered into theological controversy with the monumental mind of Augustine of Hippo, around A.D. 400, Britain and England had always been by the best Roman standards somewhat unbiddable. Certain it is that rumblings of Reformation were first heard in the Peasants' Revolt and in the English John Wyclif's writings (including his translation of the

---

* The Appendix to my book, *The Church and Music* (Duckworth, 1967) contains a number of examples of attempts on the part of church authorities to limit the exuberance of church music. Every one was unsuccessful.

Bible) well before 1400. Without any doubt one sees a touch of this independence and doggedness in the way English choral music developed.

In *The Treasury of English Church Music* volume I there are 37 choral pieces from between 1100 and 1500, and the very able introductions to each piece provided by Denis Stevens, the editor, are sufficient for most people's needs. What one sees here is a development from a very simple two-part interlude attached to a plainsong hymn tune (No. 1) to the full flowering of medieval music in John Taverner. No. 3 in that collection is *Sumer is icumen in* set to a religious text, *Perspice Christicola,* and this provides our first important clue. The interaction between secular and sacred music was inevitable once sacred music had accepted a polyphonic style. It was easy for church music to be wholly distinguishable from secular music while it was unaccompanied, monodic and unmetrical, as plainsong was. But just as people who went to church did not necessarily forget the music they heard there, but took it out with them, so the quality of secular music could not be wholly hidden from the clerics. And it has been shown fairly recently by such authorities as Dom Gregory Murray and Joseph Gelineau that there was always, and not only after the Reformation, a tendency for plainsong to be adapted to the dance rhythms of secular music. This is another way in which it did not necessarily always sound like Solesmes. It would, of course, have been regarded by purists as a corruption of sacred music when it was assimilated to secular rhythms: but the very first piece in *TECM* I gives the interlude a clear triple rhythm, and the same obviously is true of *Sumer is icumen in.**

Sumer, by the way, is strictly not a canon but a *rondellus*—twelve two-bar tunes over a two-bar ground bass of *pes.*† Naturally it can be sung as a canon but it is really a kind of primitive *passacaglia.*

Here is another clue. Ground-bass, generating variation-form, is very common in this early music. It is associated with the fact that choral music of this period is often built on, or wrapped round, a pre-existent tune—sacred or secular. No. 5 in *TECM* I, *Epiphaniam Domino Canamus* (1310) is a very interesting example of

---

* See Gregory Murray, *Gregorian Chant* (L. J. Cary, 1963), J. Gelineau, *Chant et Musique dans le Culte Chrétien* (Paris, Editions Fleurie, 1962).

† See F. Ll. Harrison, Music in Medieval Britain, 1958.

choral music finding its wings. It is based on a 14-bar *cantus* taken from an Epiphany Sequence, and is essentially a setting of a five-stanza hymn. It is for three voices, the lowest of which sticks to the *cantus firmus* so far as notes go. But neither it nor either of the other two voices sing words throughout. Some of the time they are vocalizing on some such sound as 'ah'. For example, in stanza 1, if one regards each line of words as a section, then in section 1 the chorus, or main body on singers, on the lowest line, sings phrase 1 of the cantus, Tenor I sings what we can call counterpoint A, Tenor II sings counterpoint B. Words come from the chorus: the other two vocalize. In section 2, the chorus sings line 2 (same music as line 1); Tenor II sings counterpoint A, Tenor III takes a new counterpoint—C. Then there are four bars of cadence, followed by a bar's rest. Section 3 follows; here the chorus vocalizes its *cantus,* Tenor I sings the words to counterpoint D (new tune), Tenor II vocalizes counterpoint E. For section 4, the chorus drones on in the tune we are now hearing for the fourth time, Tenor II sings words to counterpoint D, and Tenor I takes off vocalizing on counterpoint F.

And so on. Vocalizing is differently distributed in the succeeding verses, and we soon come on some 'hocketing', the word coined to indicate the breaking-up of vocalized lines by rests, which of course give the vocalization a very pungent sense of rhythm. In the third stanza we get an entertaining distribution of words, the Tenor I singing words at two or three times the speed at which the *cantus* is giving out quite other words (a technique modern listeners will associate with Gilbert and Sullivan). In the final stanza the hockets and vocalizations of the two Tenors, who have now given up hope of singing words at all, have an almost Bach-like stride, which defies description and insists on quotation:

Towards the end of the fourteenth century we begin to encounter composers whose names, though not whose dates, are identifiable. Such are Queldryk, first name unknown, who may have lived in Yorkshire, John Excetre (Exeter) who was a member of the Chapel Royal 1374–96, Oliver (first name unknown, everything else except a mass unknown too), Thomas Damett, Rector of Stockton, Wilts from 1413, died 1437, Lionel Power, who lived at Canterbury and died there in 1445 and John Dunstable, one of the giants of this age, who died in 1453. Later

(bars 85-92)

come Walter Frye, who like Dunstable spent much of his life on the Continent and was known to have joined a London musicians' guild in 1456, William Cornysh, Master of the children of the Chapel Royal, 1509–23, Robert Fayrfax, 1464–1521 (the first whose birth date is certain) another Gentleman of the Chapel Royal, Robert Carver the early sixteenth-century Scottish composer, and John Taverner, who is usually regarded as the last of the medievals.

Such musicians as these placed their talents at the disposal of the church music foundations that would use them: the abbeys, cathedrals and in particular the Chapel Royal. This last institution, whose records go back to 1135, is the longest-running church music institution in Britain of whose records we can be certain, and it is properly the name not of a building but of a singing body. (The 'chapel' went to York in the days of King John and to France in those of Henry V: that simply meant that the singers travelled, not that the building was moved.) Royal patronage of church music was, when church music needed it most, generous and fruitful.

Two other pieces from this period call for special mention. Dunstable's *Veni Sancte Spiritus* (*TECM* I 28) carries the technique of variation right into the territory of 'development'. Using the text of *Veni Sancte*, the Sequence for Pentecost written probably by Stephen Langton (*d*. 1228), he uses, not the tune associated with it but the tune we now associate with the older Pentecost text, *Veni Creator Spiritus*. (That tune is older than the Pentecost text and began with other associations, but by Dunstable's time it will certainly have suggested that hymn to the hearer.) Not the most illiterate of choirmasters would choose this tune for *Veni sancte*—the metres could not well be more different. What does Dunstable do? He uses *Veni Creator* as a sonorous bass, giving it no words and almost certainly hoping that it might be played on an instrument. (The primitive organs then available would be able to play one note at a time at the speed he wants, which is very broad.) The top voice of the three in the choral part leads off with a reference to the tune (sharpening the fourth note); what follows in that voice is hardly more than a very remote reminiscence of the rest of the tune; the other two voices provide counterpoint, mostly in a broader rhythm than the cavortings of the upper voice. At bar 91 the whole rhythm changes from what we call 3/4 to a broad 3/2, and the inner parts become more excited. One very remarkable passage comes in the lowest voice at '*hostem repellas longius*' where just before the third word the voice leaps up a major sixth: word-painting, of course; that interval was about as familiar then as a rising minor ninth would be in a modern bass part, and it is found more in English than in Continental music of this period (but very rarely even here). All this time the under voices are singing the text of *Veni Creator* (not its tune) while the top voice is cheerfully carrying on with *Veni Sancte*. At bar 121 the *tempo prino* comes back, and a new reference to the *Veni Creator* tune; just before the end the enterprising lowest voice has a leap up of an octave on '*Filium*'—with a rest after the first syllable, followed four bars later by the same leap, and a leap back down again. It is all exceedingly entertaining and ingenious, and it is an open defiance of one of the church authorities' favourite objections to musical ingenuities—the singing of more than one text at the same time. It is a technique we do not find again until Britten's *Hymn to St Peter,* in which Latin and English are heard together.

The other piece which nobody should miss is, of course, Taverner's Mass, *Westron Wynde,* of which the *Agnus Dei* is at

TECM I 36. A glance at this one movement gives some idea of the technical dexterity of the whole work. The *cantus firmus* here is a secular ballad—the music of two fourteen-syllable lines is all that Taverner uses, although mostly he repeats the second phrase. This tune appears nine times in each of the four movements of his Mass, and in the *Agnus,* three times in each of the three sub-sections. Bars 20 and 34, out of the total of 104, are the only ones in which no part of the tune is heard. The way in which he modifies the rhythm, or the opening note to produce what could almost be called a 'tonal answer', or, at one point, the octave leap in the tune (f-f) to a leap from F♯ to F, to accommodate the tonality, shows an unerring instinct for musical rhetoric. This is generally agreed to be the crown of the pre-Reformation musical repertory, because where so much of the earlier music has awkward sounds, or is ingenious at the expense of true aesthetic, this piece is, in every bar, mature and poised, incredibly difficult though in places it turns out to be.

A study of this kind of music, which thanks to modern scholars can now be quite extensive, shows music coming of age with all the coltish gawkiness of the teenager, and all the teenager's purposefulness. It really can be said that every possible experiment had been made by Taverner's time: experiments in polyphonic rhythms, clashing tonalities, and occasional word-painting. Perhaps the one that is most likely to be overlooked is that which was consequent on the virtual banning of instruments, apart from the organ, in church. Music was waiting for instruments—that is, it was waiting for the chance to say what it had to say without being tied to words. Now when we consider how very little use has ever been made by the Church of non-verbal music, one finds this the more surprising when so clearly music was clamouring for this kind of expression in the late Middle Ages. Later years brought, of course, the Organ Masses, the great Preludes of Bach and his predecessors, the Church sonatas of Mozart, and such instrumental interludes as the celebrated and immortal one in Beethoven's Mass in D: and the reason why, apart from the eighteenth-century 'Middle Voluntary', protestantism did not favour instrumental music was because of its special devotion to the Word. As for other cultures, there came to be enough instrumental music elsewhere for it not to be missed too much in church. But in the fourteenth and fifteenth centuries the vocalizings and the hockets—indeed, long before that, the vocalizings at the end of the liturgical Alleluias which generated the Sequences (for which see any book on hymnology)—were the effort of music to break away from words in an age and environment in which there was no other way for music to do it. The only alternative was secular dance and ballad. On this showing, it is understandable that the efforts of authority to check these developments were fruitless. In the end, one could say, religious opinion scored the doubtful victory of driving 'absolute' music out of church altogether, apart from what the organist may play furtively while the congregation gathers for prayer or frustratedly while it chatters its way out of church.

So much for professional church music. What of the ordinary worshipper? As has been sufficiently indicated, he had nothing to do at worship but watch, listen and pray. Medieval hymnody was as professional as the rest of church music: the Office hymns for the daily offices, at Mass, only the Sequences on high days. Psalmody was the pivot of praise at Mass, and this was done, with antiphons, to the Gregorian plainsong which, varying slightly now from one stream of tradition to another, remains familiar. As for the hymns, the *English Hymnal* gives the most generous allowance of medieval hymnody, and it can be studied there. The 'Office hymns' are to be thought of as part of the 'office' (routine) of daily worship performed by the staff of the abbey church, or the parish choir if there was one; 'offices' are appropriate to weekdays, being services in the traditional cycle that punctuated the religious life—Matins (before sunrise), Prime (sunrise), Terce (mid-morning), Next (noon), None (afternoon), Vespers (evening), and Compline (late at night). Office hymns also were provided for the chief seasons of the church's year, and for the Saints' Days. The Sequences (EH 10, 22, 130, 155, 172, 317, 351), composed at various times from the tenth century onwards (first in prose—EH 494 being an English version of the earliest known, but not providing its tune—then in verse right down to the last of them, *Dies Irae*) would be heard only on the great festivals.

No, the plain man's church music was, and had to be, the carol. Upon this I have ventured to write in my book *The English Carol* (1958); all that needs to be said here is that what we now call carols fall into two main groups: the true sacred ballads which people sang, not usually in the liturgy but on extra-liturgical occasions in or out of church, and the 'professional' carols, which were sung at Christmas time as an adornment to worship, but sung by the choirs and composed very much in the style of the simpler forms of the music we were looking at earlier. *Musica Britannica*, Vol. IV, contains a good collection of these. Along with such things must be mentioned local and dramatic songs like the famous 'Prose of the Ass' (*Orientibus Partibus*—tune at EH 129) which was sung at Sens when a procession went through the streets commemorating the flight of the Holy Family into Egypt, and songs that went with Mystery Plays, such as the Coventry Carol, and the Carol of the Nuns of Chester (OBC 22, 67). Beyond even this were the *Laudi Spirituali,* the ecstatic songs of the strange enthusiastic sects which flourished from the mid-thirteenth century onwards in southern Europe. The hymn 'Come down, O love divine' (EH 152) is translated from one of these, and the tune *Alta Trinita Beata* (EH 184) is transcribed, in a fairly unscrupulous late eighteenth-century fashion, from another. But whether any of this is, within the meaning of our brief, 'church music', is doubtful.

What really does tell us of the kind of music that was sung in choirs in England at the end of the Middle Ages is the contents of those two priceless collections, the *Eton Choir Book* and the *Old Hall Manuscript*. These, preserved respectively at Eton College and at Old Hall, Ware (England) are the bases from which most modern scholarly transcriptions have come; other such sources are mentioned in detail in the introduction to *TECM* I. On the evidence of such sources we can safely say that if there was one age in which 'church music' was clearly distinguishable from any other kind of music, and at the same time positively leading the way, far ahead in ingenuity and imagination of any other kind of music, it was the late Middle Ages.

2. A CRISIS OF CULTURES, 1532–1649

The story of English church music in the time of the English Reformation is the most impressive vindication in all history of our thesis that church authority has no means of stemming the flow of music. We remarked earlier that the first great period of English music runs uninterruptedly from Dunstable to Gibbons. To look at this great volume of music as a single *corpus*, one would have no idea that a Reformation had happened, except perhaps to infer something of the kind from the appearance of English texts in the liturgical settings. But the fact was that more attempts were made, from more directions, to control music's means of expression than at any other time from Pope John XXII to the present day. It will indeed be part of our argument, the rest of which we shall have to save for our last chapter, that music cannot ever be corrupted or thwarted by authoritative prohibition: it can only be corrupted by the wrong kind of encouragement.

It is the measure of the perverse genius of King Henry VIII that he was able single-handed to engineer the reformation of the English Church; it is the measure of that 'consummate statesmanship' which is attributed to him in the *Dictionary of National Biography* that he could, in 1521, earn the title from the Pope of 'Defender of the Faith' for his tract *Assertio Septem Sacramentorum* attacking Luther, and little more than ten years later could in defiance of that same papal authority constitute himself 'supreme Head' of the Church of England. One cannot say he was influenced by anybody—such an assertion in his lifetime would have probably cost you your head. He took note of what had happened in Europe—no more than that. The new church was his church—he virtually thought of himself as its inventor and its owner. Only a massive combination of first-class intellect and shameless tyranny could have accomplished what he did. Within the fairly short space of fifteen years he had ordered the dissolution of the monasteries and the reorganization of the English dioceses, and the first drafts of the theological constitution of the new English church. Though he did not write most of it, his mind is behind *The King's Book* (1543), a revision of an earlier manifesto, *The Bishops' Book* (1536), and in his edition of this document T. A. Lacey said of Henry that he was 'a stubbornly

Catholic King who had a personal quarrel with the Pope'. He adds, 'Henry's quarrel was made up within thirty years by his daughter Mary'. True though this is, he did not add that the quarrel was reopened five years later than that by Queen Elizabeth I and her advisers. No: the Church of England was here to stay from the time of King Henry, and the Catholic interlude of Queen Mary's five years was no more than that: so decisive was Henry's work, and that of his advisers and sympathizers who carried it on in the reign of Edward VI. A vernacular liturgy was first fully authorized in 1549; an English Bible had been in use since 1538.

But it was something very different from politics that brought pressure to bear on church music. It was, indeed, nascent puritanism. That is a word which should be used with caution: but it will do here because it seems first to have come into currency in 1564, to describe an attitude which was to become a very influential body of opinion. Once a word has been coined to describe such a body of opinion you can safely guess that that opinion has been in currency for at least a generation. What is properly called puritanism had actually been in the air for considerably longer than that.

For puritanism is nothing less that the sanctification of humanism. Such a statement should shock nobody, even though many are led to believe that puritanism and humanism are directly opposed. We must explain this as briefly as we can.

The Reformation is usually spoken of in theological terms. It is better understood as a natural consequence of the Renaissance. For what really was Luther's protest about? It was against the Church's insistence on treating grown people as children. It was a manifesto for maturity. If he protested against indulgences, against bureaucratic complexities in the Church, against theological obscurities, he was saying 'Treat Christians as grown men and women: do not any longer insist that they are not to be trusted with the Bible, that they need a priestly system to introduce them to the presence of God, that they need to pass examinations like schoolchildren in order to be admitted to God's favour'. 'Justification by Faith' had that complaint at its centre. The maturity which the whole of that amorphous cataclysm we call the Renaissance was claiming, the Reformers were claiming as well. But so had many before them. So had John Hus, who was burnt as a heretic in 1415. So had Wyclif: so had the organizers of the English Peasant's Revolt. And so, in his way, did King Henry VIII, who his reasons being admittedly discreditable but had they not been those reasons and that king they might well have been others) insisted that the Pope could not treat all Christians any longer as his children. For the Reformers, Mother Church and the Holy Father were due for superannuation.

The corollary was that mature men and women could organize their own relationships with God. Now this was all very well. Neither Luther nor Henry really believed that, nor did John Calvin in Geneva. The only people who did believe it were the Brownists, the ancestors of the later Congregationalists, who (like the Quakers when they formed themselves into a recognizable body of opinion in the 1650s) really did attempt to set up a church order in which God could speak directly to a Christian body of people. But the world was not quite ready for that. Luther believed most assuredly in a church system, episcopal in form, which, while ridding itself of the aspects of Catholic order he found objectionable, kept some control over the faithful. Henry's beliefs were similar, except that he vested that control ultimately in the Crown. But plenty of influential and lively-minded people were taking a more radical line, and finding ways by which they could claim that the Church has no human head, its only Head being Christ. And such people were feared and loathed by such as Luther and King Henry quite as much as the Pope. For if you remove the earthly Father from his place of authority, and hand over that authority to the Crown, or to the bishops led by an archbishop, you will regard anybody who disputes those new authorities as a security risk—which is exactly what did happen in England towards the end of the sixteenth century when the Fleet prison in London suddenly accommodated a number of prisoners on charges of treason, some of whom were Roman Catholics who refused to abjure their allegiance, others of whom were Brownists who, disputing the right of Archbishop Whitgift to rule the Church, were regarded as committing treason to the Queen.

All this was the consequence of claiming the rights of maturity.

Those who make that claim are often youthful, and truculent, impatient and arrogant: but nobody can stop them making the claim. Now our purpose in going into all this is so that the reader may be prepared for that aspect of the puritan, maturity-claiming, excellence-seeking habit of mind which especially bore on the musicians. For another field in which people were claiming maturity was the intellectual: and in making their claim here they were just as clumsy as they were elsewhere. The centre of this was the new status of the Scriptures which the Reformation accorded them.

So long as the Bible is a book in Latin which you receive through priestly interpretation but never consider reading critically yourself, you remain a passive receiver of what it says (or what the priests say it says). If you begin to read it in your own language, you are in a new situation—one in which you begin to say, 'The Bible says' where you used to say, 'The Church says'. You still regard it as an inspired and holy book: but just because it is now within your reach you approach it with a new mixture of dread and audacity. Ronald Knox shrewdly observed, of the Reformers' zeal for the vernacular Scriptures, 'The whole Reformation was the apotheosis of the learned clerk; you might not read *your* Bible, you must read Luther's Bible or Cranmer's as the case might be. . . . It must have been an awkward moment for Luther when he discovered that men who attracted a large following in Germany were deriving their inspiration from the Bible, and reading a great deal more into it than he did. There was only one course left to him, . . . he must appeal from the claim to a living inspiration to the dead letter of the Bible as it stood. Thenceforward simple people . . . were to be guided by the Scripture as interpreted by Luther, and Calvin, and Zwingli, and Beza and Knox—by the pundits.'* That was where the claim to maturity defeated itself; for it was on biblical grounds, but on the grounds of the Bible interpreted by a certain body of opinion, that restrictions were placed on the use of music in church services. That body of opinion was, compared with what prevailed in the Middle Ages, word-oriented. Mysticism was suspected: imagination was regarded as dangerous. It was the literal word that counted.

* R. A. Knox, *Enthusiasm* (1950) pp. 115, 134–5.

Whence else can have come the Genevan insistence, imitated in Britain, that congregational singing must be confined to metrical Psalms and such other passages of Scripture as were admitted to be songs? Luther himself believed in hymnody—if pressed he would probably have had to admit that what he believed in was the 37 hymns he himself wrote—as a proper exercise for mature Christians. In hymnody they can sing of their New Testament faith. But Luther's *Christ Lag in Todesbanden* is not, on the fundamentalist opinion which had so rapidly followed the Reformation, 'in the Bible' in the sense that the Psalms are. Calvin, in prescribing psalmody in Geneva, was as Catholic as the medievals who used only psalmody at the Mass, but for very different reasons. Calvin was fortunate in getting them translated by good poets and set to music by an incomparable musical editor, Louis Bourgeois, whose tunes (or arrangements) in the 1551 *Octante-Trois Pseaulmes* (commonly called the Genevan Psalter) are the very foundation of all English hymnody. The English were less fortunate, in being tied down to Thomas Sternhold's ballads; the choice of the ballad metre for the English Psalter (which like the Genevan was completed in 1562) was unhappy, since the metre that sings so well when it is telling a story of kings and battles and chivalry sits less easily on the profundities of Christian devotion. At any rate the colleagues of Sternhold who after his death in 1549 completed the Psalter did not do it very well, almost certainly because they were not composing freely but manhandling the words of the Psalter until they could fit them into the metre of the old ballads. The same is true of the Scottish Psalter of 1564, and of that of 1650 which is still in use in Scotland. It is not literature, but a fundamentalist carpentering of words already regarded as sacred because they are 'in the Bible'. Only the genius of the musicians, who produced those incomparable miniatures, the common metre psalm tunes of England and Scotland, saved the whole enterprise from complete cultural collapse.

But before we slip into the familiar cliché which says that all puritan opinion is repressive of the arts, there is one statement which will serve to correct the historical skid. This is that the puritan opinion we are dealing with here was exceedingly sensitive about what happened *in church*; it is a mistake to extend that opinion to the rest of life. And the sensitiveness to what went on in church was the result of a new kind of thinking about what the church, at public worship, was for. Two streams joined to form this opinion. One was that all worship was public worship: the suppression of monastic foundations meant the discontinuance, except for pockets of resistance or private Catholic chapels which somehow escaped the censors, of the offices. The Church at worship was the people at worship. The second stream tended to say that the Church was there to instruct. Worship was not, in the medieval mind, so much a classroom as a theatre. The puritans said that the *mind* was indeed the part of a Christian that was most likely to need constant vigilance and correction. There was, indeed, much in Thomas Goodwin's famous dictum, 'our worst sins are sins of the mind': the value of that proposition is perhaps more apparent in the present anti-intellectual climate than it has been for three centuries since he first made it in the 1650s. When the Church was on parade, therefore, it must not throw dust in the eyes of worshippers by indulging in aesthetic extravagances.

What went on in the only other community recognized by advanced puritan opinion, the home, was something quite different. The home was the other focus of the religious pattern. Let us celebrate once again the sonorous amplitude of the title-page of Sternhold and Hopkins:

THE

WHOLE BOOK

OF

PSALMS

Collected into

English Metre

BY

Thomas Sternhold, John Hopkins

And Others

Conferred with the HEBREW

Set forth and allowed to be sung in all Churches, of all the People together, before and after Morning and Evening Prayer, and also before and after Sermons; and moreover in private Houses, for their godly Solace and Comfort, laying apart all ungodly Songs and Ballads, which tend only to the nourishing of Vice and corrupting of Youth.

James V. 13

If any be afflicted, let him pray: And if any be merry let him sing Psalms.

Colossians III.16

Let the Word of God dwell plenteously in you, in all Wisdom, teaching and exhorting one another in Psalms, Hymns and Spiritual Songs, singing unto the Lord in your Hearts.

It is all there: the Biblical foundation ('conferred with the HEBREW', and the authoritative texts below), the joining of church and home as the places of worship, and the exhortation against triviality in amusement.

Following this, the musical psalters were from the first issued in harmonized editions (Day's of 1563, one year after the publication of the original complete psalter with melodies) for use at home. Successive editions, often contributed to by the ablest musicians of the day, continued to appear throughout the puritan period, the most celebrated being Daman's *Psalter,* 1591, Este's, 1592, Ravenscroft's, 1621 and Playford's, 1671 and 1677: in Scotland Miller's of 1635 was the most able of the harmonized versions. Este in 1592 used ten of the best-known madrigalists of his day for his harmonizations, including John Farmer, Thomas Morley, George Kirbye and John Dowland. Ravenscroft drew on these and by using composers of the later generation brought his total of contributors. excluding himself, to 22. All those of whom any parallel record is left were good contemporary composers. To these we can add private collections using texts other than that of the official Psalter, like those of Hunnys and Leighton (not to mention the ineffable versification of *The Acts* set to music by Christopher Tye back in 1553 or the equally crude Psalter version by Archbishop Matthew Parker for which Tallis wrote his celebrated series of eight tunes, about 1560).

It is easily demonstrable the puritans liked chamber music and had little use for sociable music or for concert music (even of such a kind as was available then). And for a series of well-chosen quotations from leading exponents of this kind of opinion who sought to restrain music in church, the reader should consult Chapter 2 of Peter le Huray's excellent book, *Music and the Refor-*

mation in England, 1549–1660.* What immediately follows here summarizes what can be extensively read there.

The phrase which gives the clue to the whole movement in the period 1558–1600 is in the Injunctions of Queen Elizabeth I, 1559: ' . . . and that there be a modest distinct song, so used in all parts of the common prayers in the Church, that the same may be plainly understood, as if it were read without singing, and yet nevertheless, for the comforting of such as delight in music, it may be permitted that in the beginning, or in the end of common prayers either at morning or evening, there may be sung a Hymn, or such like song. . . .' 'Modest and distinct'—that is the key phrase. This was a royal pronouncement, the end-product of plenty of debate, and the Queen was neither a tyrant nor a philistine about the arts. But the one thing required is modesty and distinctness, 'that the same may be plainly understood'. Understanding—the one great Reformation commandment, is associated with congregational participation, the other which is like unto it. (It is to be understood that 'Hymn' here certainly means a metrical psalm, or one of the canticles appended to the psalms in the official version: nothing else.)

Such an injunction can be interpreted positively or negatively—either 'let us have music and keep it modest' or 'virtually all music is immodest and indistinct'—according to the critic's temperament. It was not long before the sterner voice was heard criticizing popish ceremonies as conducted in the Queen's private chapel: the Dean of St Paul's (Nowell) made that point in a sermon in 1563 and the Queen exercised the royal prerogative of telling him to talk about something else or be silent. She had, anyhow, her own political reasons at that time for not appearing to be too violently anti-Catholic.

Presumably, then, she did not take too literally the opinion expressed in the *Book of Homilies* (1563) that non-congregational singing ought to be discouraged.

Writing later about this period, an unknown writer in the reign of James I comments that in many places funds originally designed for the maintenance of choirs were diverted to the establishment of 'lectures': that is another prominent puritan

* Barrie & Jenkins (Studies in Church Music) 1967.

signal. The *minds* need nourishing, and the appointment of 'lecturers' in certain parishes was encouraged—these being men whose special duty it was to preach at greater length and depth than the ordinary worship demanded—to deepen people's intellectual apprehension of the Faith. More important, this, than music.

A ban on contrapuntal music at Winchester Cathedral (1571) points the same way: what is sung contrapuntally will be less readily understood, and may draw attention unduly to the skill of composer or singer.

If this was the sort of opinion that was being put about, it is not surprising that musicians became socially and morally depressed. Economists say that money was worth half in 1600 what it was worth in 1550: that was an age of inflation (later ages can cap that story). But certainly musicians found themselves getting nearer and nearer the bottom of the economic heap; they were underpaid and undervalued. Dr le Huray* quotes a series of indictments and charges against church musicians from a document drawn up in Wells, and covering the years 1591–1609. This lists three charges of fornication, one each of absenteeism, failure to take communion three times in a year, gambling, and keeping an alehouse, and three general reminders of the need for faithful church attendance and the thrice-yearly communion. In nineteen years that is not, human nature being what it is, too formidable a list of charges, but this is the sort of thing puritan opinion made a great thing of. It was agreeable to people of that mind to depress others' standards of living and then blame them for taking their pleasure where they could find it; it is not easy to see how a vicar-choral in those days could take the Church very seriously.

But when we have said all that—this is the great age of English Tudor music. What a fantastic contradiction that is! Where do Tallis, Byrd, Tomkins and Morley fit into this picture?

William Byrd (1543–1623) is always acknowledged to be the greatest English composer of his generation. Second to him, and a generation earlier, is Thomas Tallis (*c.* 1505–85). In the music of these, and of their many eminent contemporaries, we find a poise and assurance which perhaps even the greatest of the pre-

* *op. cit.* pp. 41–2.

Reformation composers hardly achieved. In any work of Byrd or Tallis that the ordinary reader is likely to hear there is a combination of pellucid clarity and muscial wit which shows that English music had really by now found its true form. Such miniatures as Byrd's *Sacerdotes Domini, Iustorum Animae* and *Ave Verum* repay attention to every note and every chord. Tallis composed far less music for English words than Byrd, and probably his *If ye love me* is the only English piece of his likely to be familiar to most readers, though in the astonishing forty-part motet *Spem in alium* Tallis showed that his sheer skill was something that the most ingenious of the fifteenth-century composers would have respected.

But the plain fact is that if one looks through the very good selection of music from this period in the second volume of the *Treasury of English Church Music* one sees very clearly how the principles of the Reformation were turned to the best uses by the best composers. If we except the last two pieces in that source, all the rest of the music seems to display the quality of the 'modest and distinct song' without losing any part of its musical integrity.

Byrd is at the centre of this because of his very large output, and because he composed music with equal success for both Latin and English words. This in itself is interesting. His chief biographer, E. H. Fellowes* justly observes that his later English pieces (1611) are more successful than the earlier set (1588–9); and one cannot but feel that a composer who was accustomed to the sound of Latin would confront the new English rite with the same kind of misgiving that some contemporary composers feel when required to set the new English rites of our own time.

However—Byrd and Tallis are special cases. Tallis was already something like 65 when the Elizabethan Settlement was finally drawn up in 1570. Byrd was only 37. Tallis had already become an honoured musician for his settings of Latin texts. Byrd had been organist of Lincoln Cathedral since 1562. They met at professional level when Byrd was sworn in as a Gentleman of the Chapel Royal in 1572, where Tallis was the incumbent music-director; and they shared the duties for a time. Thus they were both in the royal favour, and in 1575 they were jointly granted a licence to publish sacred music, which was a very special mark of

* *William Byrd,* Oxford University Press, 1936: p. 138).

royal patronage. Only a few people held such a licence (one of these had been John Day, who published the first four-part edition of the Sternhold and Hopkins Psalter in 1563). And this was to a large measure the secret of Byrd's success: for on Tallis's death (1585) the licence remained with Byrd, and under it he proceeded to put out several series of works which have become acknowledged as masterpieces: the two series of *Cantiones Sacrae* (1575, revised 1589, and 1591: 61 pieces in all), the *Gradualia* (1605, 1607, 78 items including the three mentioned above), the English anthems in two series (1589, 1611), the *Short* and *Great* Services, and other service music.

Byrd was an avowed Catholic sympathizer; his wife was cited for the technical offence of recusancy (refusing to conform to the new anglican settlement) in 1577 and he himself was so cited in 1586; but neither of them was ever punished for what brought several Catholic priests to the fate of martyrdom. It was royal patronage that protected them in the reign of Elizabeth, and after that time Byrd was too distinguished a layman to suffer any sort of persecution in a new reign in which less political anxiety was in any case shown over the issue. And all this output of cathedral music (for that is what it exclusively was) went on in the face of the puritan discouragements, partly because Byrd had the right to publish it and partly because of his association with the Chapel Royal which obstinately refused to be bound by the restrictions urged upon so many other centres of church music.

It was indeed the Chapel Royal which gave their chance to several other leading composers of the time, among them Thomas Morley, Nathaniel Giles, John Bull, and (of the next generation) Thomas Tomkins and Orlando Gibbons. Those others whose work has been preserved were all associated with cathedral foundations—Mundy of Windsor, Hilton of Cambridge, Weelkes of Winchester and Chichester, Batten of Winchester, Amner of Ely.

The music of these composers is a country in which it would be delightful to linger. Here we must be content to mention Morley and Gibbons as perhaps the most distinguished composers apart from Byrd. Morley is plausibly regarded as the inventor of the Verse Anthem—a musical form which provides a direct link between the Tudor style and that of the Restoration; as we shall see in a moment, they have precious little else in common. His best-known anthem, 'Out of the Deep' (*TECM* II p. 114) is a verse anthem dating, one supposes from the 1590s, and in a short life (1557–1603) he managed to make himself the pioneer of English madrigals and the author of the most comprehensive book on music theory up to that time published in English, the *Plaine and Easie Introduction to Practicall Musicke;*

Orlando Gibbons (1583–1625) was similarly short-lived and energetic; he is the best-known name in Tudor music nowadays not least because of the eleven hymn tunes from his appendix to George Wither's collection of hymns (1623) which were revived by the *English Hymnal*. Gibbons, who stands at the end of the period, makes it possible for us to insist that although in the end this style gave way to another and very different style, it showed, in its latest manifestations, no sign whatever of degeneration. There is an imaginative sweep about *Hosanna to the Son of David* which shows a masterful sureness of touch, and an intellectual solidity in that quite remarkable piece preserved at *TECM* II p. 198, 'See, See, the Word is incarnate' (a work which should be heard oftener) worthy of the best in this tradition. Gibbons emerges perhaps as the supreme melodist of this great company. It needed a certain kind of imagination, in which he excelled, to conceive the opening phrases of pieces so different in style as 'The Silver Swan', 'Hosanna to the Son of David' and 'O Lord, in thy wrath' (*TECM* II p. 191). His hymn tunes show in a different way what a master of melody he was.

It seems that, although the condition of church musicians was far from comfortable in the sixteenth century, with the turn of the next, things improved a little. The fortunes of the Chapel Royal seem to have prospered and its endowments became more generous. This would be because of the rise within the Church of England of what is loosely called a 'high church' party. That cannot mean what is meant in the early twentieth century; it rather means to distinguish between those who were sure that the Church, in its public behaviour, should exhibit some sense of style and occasion, and those who were more concerned to suppress extravagance. One of music's chief benefactors in the early seventeenth century was the archetypal 'high churchman', Archbishop Laud, whose open quarrel with the puritans became an historic landmark.

Not but what the puritans themselves were becoming more articulate: and, what was more alarming for the higher reaches of church music-making, more powerful. Soon after 1620 there was a famous lawsuit in Durham, in which a senior prebendary, Peter Smart, attempted to take the canons to court for disobeying the Injunctions of 1559 by introducing complex and learned music instead of the 'modest and distinct song.' One of the leaders of the movement which so incensed the prebendary was John Cosin, later bishop of that see, and author of the famous translation of *Veni Creator* which begins 'Come, Holy Ghost, our souls inspire'. Not much later the notorious William Prynne (he who so eloquently objected to stage plays) delivered himself of an attack on complex music in church, and another pamphleteer, William Bastwick, in language lurid even by the standards of early seventeenth-century journalism, belaboured the cathedral authorities for extravagant expenditure on what he regarded as trifles—which included music. As for the attitude of Cromwell, the behaviour he condoned in his soldiers in the ancient churches of England speaks for itself.

The pe.. od we are here discussing ended in a civil war, and in the beheading of the English sovereign. For eleven years after that the country was ruled by a puritan parliament with a puritan leader of monumental ability and ferocious religious convictions: and for a while even the most ardent and skilful of composers would have been discouraged from writing anything of consequence. During the period of Cromwell's ascendancy, say between 1640 and 1658, every effort was made to turn the country into what would now be called a Presbyterian or Congregationalist network of churches, with the extrusion from their pulpits of incumbents and dignitaries who did not see things the puritan way. This conflagration was the end-product of the mounting dispute between the two ways of looking at religion; a puritan view which is always, at its best, no more than a plea for maturity, excellence and personal modesty, became in the hands of the fanatics a riot of iconoclasm, while the older view, at its best contemplative, imaginative and hospitable to beauty, became a charter for snobbery and the self-protection of the ill-educated wealthy.

But the truth about all this is more clearly expounded in the Church's music than in any of the Church's documents. If one in fact listens to 'Lord, for thy tender mercies' sake' (probably Hilton: *TECM* II p. 48), 'Hide not thou thy face' (Farrant, *TECM* II p. 46), 'Terra Tremuit' (Byrd) or 'When David heard' (Tomkins), not to mention the verse anthems and service settings of the period, the message comes through loud and clear that music cannot be arrested in its development by authority, though often it can be assisted. Authority, even in the rather negative form of calvinist intellectualism, demanded clarity and intelligibility. In any of the simple anthems of this period this is what it got. Authority could not arrest an artist's desire to interpret and illuminate; indeed, authority insisted on precisely that from its preachers and lecturers. This also is what it got from those English musicians who developed so delicate a pictorial touch in their interpretations of words (like the openings of Byrd's *Justorum Animae* and *Terra Tremuit* and those points of genius we have referred to in Gibbons). If authority seemed, on the negative side, to be oppressively dogmatic, some of its censures could be positively interpreted by the patient as saying, 'We want you to *communicate*'; and if we rightly interpret the response of the great Tudor composers in this way, then it was this that gave them the quality we recognize as 'English', Nobody will mistake a motet of Byrd for one of Palestrina. You could say, as people often do, that there is no more *English* piece of music in existence than Byrd's *Haec Dies*. It is, historically, the English puritan genius that wants to communicate and to edify; the English theologian who wants to interpret even more than to assemble knowledge; the English listener (to sermons or motets) who wants to understand. What in other spheres was an ugly and philistine repression was interpreted by English musicians as a kind of liberation.

One name, perhaps more familiar to ordinary churchgoers than any of those above mentioned, must be celebrated here: it is that of a musician who falls neither into the category of the puritan psalmist nor into that of the scholarly polyphonist. This is, of course, William Merbecke. Nothing of his composition has survived apart from two Latin motets, a Mass, and the *Book of Common Prayer Noted*. But in that last-named work, he made himself a household name wherever the English rite was sung, especially during the twentieth century when the Eucharist found its way back to the centre of parish worship.

Apparently his work was little used in his own time. It consisted of the setting to music of all the singable parts of the Prayer Book rites of Morning and Evening Prayer and of the Eucharist, as set out in the 1549 Prayer Book. It was published in 1550,* and on its evidence Merbecke was the last composer of Gregorian plain-song. His principle was almost exclusively 'one syllable, one note'. Modern parish use testifies that Merbecke produced a kind of music which any parishioner can sing without the least difficulty—the apotheosis of the 'modest and distinct song'. He was an enthusiast for the new English rite and took to it as our own contemporaries have sometimes taken to the new rites of our time. Apart from the psalm tunes, this was positively the only congregational music produced in this period.

---

* This makes Peter le Huray's date of 'c. 1531' for Merbecke's birth a good deal too late. Other sources give it as c. 1510, which makes him an exact contemporary of Tallis, since both died in 1585.

3. THE NEW PROFESSIONALS, 1649–1738

It is always dangerous to generalize in historical judgment, and to overstate the sort of proposition that categorizes and labels historical periods; but if it is ever safe to do such things it is safe in speaking of the Restoration. We have emphasized that the development of English music of all kinds from its infancy to the beginning of the seventeenth century was a smooth and natural development which outside forces, even such fierce forces as those which produced the English Reformation, were unable seriously to affect. Musical talent could direct itself this way or that, set these texts or those, serve this or that form of church order and find ways of expressing itself so long as the pressures on it were propositional, and non-musical. Neither opposition nor un-fashionableness, neither economic depression nor the slender chance of ever hearing their music performed outside their immediate circles, could prevent musicians of the standing of Byrd, Weelkes and Gibbons from producing music. Only a strictly musical pressure could have diverted them from the exercise of gifts which they had inherited direct from their music ancestors. Nobody said to Byrd: 'We want no more of your kind of music because there is another kind we now prefer.' The idea would have been unintelligible.

But that really is what happened in the seventeenth century. A musical earthquake took place in Europe comparable to that caused two and a half centuries later by the explorations of Debussy and Schoenberg; it might have had a less cataclysmic effect on English music had it not been for the circumstances that immediately preceded the Restoration of the Monarchy in 1660: but rumblings of it were to be heard quite a while before that date.

The reader should if possible have at his elbow the second and third volumes of the *Treasury of English Church Music,* and of course he will eventually want to consult the companion histories that go with them, written by the same authorities who edited the texts (Peter le Huray and Christopher Dearnley) in *Studies in English Church Music;* but in case he has not, we will here transcribe the first ten bars of two pieces which stand together almost at the end of Volume 2: the first is 'O praise the Lord all ye heathen', by

Adrian Batten who was born before 1590 and died about 1637, began his working life as a pupil of Holmes, organist of Winchester Cathedral, then went to London as a lay-clerk at Westminster Abbey, later organist of St Paul's Cathedral. The second is 'Praise the Lord' by Walter Porter (*c.* 1595–1659), a Gentleman of the Chapel Royal until the temporary dissolution of its choir about 1643 (see Examples 2 and 3).

Batten (bars 1-9)

Probably less than ten years separated the dates of these two composers' births: yet the merest glance at the two pieces of music indicates that something radical has happened. What had happened was the result of the fact that whereas Batten had spent all his working life in England, Porter had spent a good deal of it in Italy.

'Praise the Lord' is a verse anthem published in 1632. Verse anthems—anthems constructed in several episodes and using solo voices—were even by that date nothing new: there are plenty

of them in the Tudor period. But rhetorical melismatic solos certainly are new, and so is figured bass, which in Italy, where it seems to have been invented around 1600, was called *basso continuo.*

This piece, which is one of the first of such compositions to come from an Englishman, must have sounded outlandish, if indeed it ever received a performance in his lifetime. A listener of puritan persuasion would have gone purple in the face.

The historical fact is, however, that what before 1660 would have been a furtive experiment became, within a few years of the new dispensation, the almost unvarying fashion. Charles II's exile in France brought him into contact with the 'new music' and at every level, after he returned, this was the musical fashion set by the top people in England.

Now any innovation so radical as this has overtones that go beyond music. The basic new idea is that of melody and accompaniment, replacing polyphony. Instruments were developing, and there could now be more for them to do than simply to double the voice parts. If now not all the responsibility for music-making fell on the voices, you could compose music which (unlike the earlier style, which although no doubt it often was accompanied, was complete music when sung *a cappella*) was incomplete without instruments.

But instruments are not yet on an equal footing with voices. They are accompaniments: they are not yet making music entirely dissociated from voice or dance. Therefore the new notion that one of the partners has priority over the other—that the voice leads, and the instrument is subject to it—intrudes into music-making. Somebody is more important than somebody else.

You might well object that in the fifteenth century the 'important' part was the *cantus firmus*, the plainsong tune or whatever other melody the rest of the singers were decorating. True: but, put in elementary terms, that meant that the people with the simplest and most familiar part to sing, the holders of those long and grave sounds which were the groundwork of the whole piece, were 'important' in the sense in which the more athletic singers of the surrounding parts were not. The new music reverses this. Here you have your athletic singer, now a soloist and abruptly being thought of as a *virtuoso* (another Italian word) catching the attention, while the accompanist is in the background—indispensable but no more obtrusive than the foundations of a building.

More than this: the composer will laboriously write out every note of the singer's part—the 'melody'—while he leaves the accompanist to fashion his part from a shorthand written in figures: only the bass will be written out: the harmony will be played in conformity with the figured indications but the actual disposition of the notes will be improvised by the player. In a modern edition an accompaniment to music of this sort will be provided by the editor (as it is in *TECM* in Porter's piece); an original score will look like what we have written out here.

Note that this is not to say that with this enormous addition to polyphony, *counterpoint disappears;* even polyphony does not disappear wholly: choral episodes will still be written polyphonically (see Porter at bars 19–28, 47–65). You can even mix the styles when a 'verse' is being sung by four soloists (bars 69–83). But whatever happens, counterpoint still prevails: the bass will be in good counterpoint with the melody. At least, that is how it is when the music is being composed at the highest level.

But of course this development makes an immense difference to the vocabulary of music, and above all to its rhetoric— its equipment for expressiveness and emphasis. The rhetoric (this word is not here used in any pejorative sense) in the Tudor composers, their word-painting and points of emphasis, are all achieved by contrapuntal and harmonic means, and by devices in which the whole singing body is involved. In the new music it is at least partly placed at the discretion of an individual singer.

It is easy to see what possibilities for degeneracy lie within so dramatic an enrichment of music's vocabulary as this. For if by any chance a composer stumbles on the temptation to write plenty of melody, but a bass that is not in good counterpoint with it, or a melody which cannot imply anything but a trivial bass, then music will certainly degenerate. For what has happened is a visual and palpable separation in music of the principles of reason and rhetoric: the rhetoric is in the melody, the rational principle in the bass. In music as in any other art, the degeneracy sets in when the balance between these two principles—which can be described analogically as the principles of freedom and discipline—is upset.

It is equally easy, and in this particular case I should insist that it is not misleading, to see the analogy between the rise of virtuoso music and the rise of the social conception of 'top people as the arbiters of culture'. It is no random coincidence that this music came into its own in environments in which the focus of society was in the Court and among the aristocracy. Give England a king who has been exposed to it, and who revels in exactly that kind of life, who reacts emphatically against the puritan suspicion of 'public style', and promotes precisely 'public style' for all he is worth, and no other kind of music will have a chance where he reigns. This is exactly what happened at the Restoration.

As a promoter, King Charles II knew what he was about. The first step in re-establishing the Chapel Royal as a centre of musical excellence was to pack off the most promising of its children to be trained by French musicians and to imbibe the atmosphere of the court of Louis XIV. *TECM* Volume 3, after three introductory numbers from the transition period, presents

Pelham Humfrey (1647–74), Michael Wise (*c.* 1648–87) and John Blow (1649–1708), to which list it is certainly proper to add the names of Thomas Tudway (*c.* 1650–1726) and William Turner (1651–1740). Take the ages of those in 1661, and you see a procession of youngsters who became significant composers, being all brought up in the new tradition, and no doubt catching the infection from Humfrey, who was sent to study in France from his seventeenth to his twentieth year. In the three examples in *TECM* III (Humfrey, p. 36, Wise, p. 49, Blow, p. 58) one sees the dramatic possibilities of the new style, and reading or hearing these pieces, which employ full choir, soloists, strings and continuo, one can readily imagine the impact they made, and the surprise they caused. One must always understand that they would be heard only in the highest reaches of church music performance: the parishes would know nothing about all this.

The Blow anthem *Salvator Mundi* mentioned above is perhaps of special interest being in the style of an accompanied motet rather than in that of a verse anthem; but the reader will note how it uses the new techniques to provide deep expressiveness—a touch of dotted rhythm, a *melisma* on 'salva nos' handed from voice to voice, and the suspensions on 'crucem'.

The English predecessors of this Restoration style, apart from Porter mentioned above, include Henry Lawes (1596–1662) and William Child (1606–97); Lawes is always worth pausing on, especially his songs, and his music for Milton's *Comus*. He had an unusual dramatic talent, and it comes out surprisingly in some of the tunes he wrote for George Sandys's private version of the Psalms, published in 1638. The *English Hymnal* has a generous selection of these (look him up in the Composers' Index), but Psalm 8 (*Whitehall*) and Psalm 72 (*Farley Castle*) are especially notable as examples of the song-writer's art, with their unusual melodic intervals and (in the second of these) in the new shape of melody, with its ending at the top of the scale. The four short pieces in *TECM* (p. 1ff) are also settings of psalms by Sandys with three voice parts and figured bass.

Matthew Locke's 'Lord, let me know mine end' (*TECM* p. 21) is an early verse anthem (he died in 1677), scored for 5-part chorus, four solo voices and figured bass (marked 'organ'). Parts of it are polyphonic: parts, both in the chorus and in the verses, are

homophonic, and the contrasts between the textures turn out to be masterly in the setting of this highly dramatic text.

After the initial 'explosion' we come swiftly to the Purcells, Daniel (*c.* 1663–1717) and his more celebrated elder brother Henry (1659–95). Henry Purcell clearly dominates over the whole group; his music was far more often played than that of the others (it is well known to have caught the attention of Charles Wesley, who was born twelve years after Purcell died). He imparts to the new music a very strong and salty individuality which is hardly to be found in any of his contemporaries, and he can use with equal facility all the devices of the new vocabulary. He is justly thought of as the most English of all these English com-

posers, and he leaves his thumbprint on his works especially in
his fascinating handling of ground bass (more found in his
secular works than in the sacred ones) and his use of a persistent
dotted-note rhythm to achieve certain effects—as in the Alleluias
at the end of his famous *Evening Hymn* (*CAB* 60). The four well-
contrasted pieces of his in *TECM* are an excellent introduction to
his style: the tender and expressive duet, 'Close thine eyes' (p.
83)—about as near the fringe of 'church music' as the *Evening
Hymn*; the 8-part unfigured 'Hear my prayer' (p. 87), harking
back to the pre-Italianate style, 'I will give thanks', which in-
troduces the instrumental 'symphony', an extended introduction,
the word also being used for instrumental interludes later in the
piece, and the very subdued homophonic fragment, 'Thou
knowest, Lord' (p. 111), for 4-part choir and organ. The
'symphony' a celebration of the availability and approved standing of a good instrumental band, is most famously present in
'Rejoice in the Lord alway' (*CAB* 77), probably the most widely
used to-day of all verse anthems, and here the provision of an introduction which has no thematic connection whatever with what
follows, and is in a different rhythm, becomes less incongruous
when one finds, as the anthem goes on, that changes of time-
signature are used with very telling effect in the various sections.
The whole of this piece is a superb study in the use of rhythms,
both in detail and as a part of the structure.

Purcell (Henry) wrote very few dull pages. Perhaps most of
those who immediately followed him were less innocent.
Christopher Dearnley, who adds a pungent critical sense to his
scholarship, unhesitatingly categorizes some of the later composers as mostly dull or at best workmanlike. Daniel, Henry
Purcell's younger brother, left little that anyone need trouble
with for long. Hine, Kempton, Kelway, Kent, Nares—these add
little to what the earlier generation had said. But there were some
bright geniuses. Jeremiah Clarke (whose Trumpet Voluntary was
for so long credited to Purcell) has some very delicate work to his
credit: his song-like psalm tunes are always attractive even when
at their most characteristic (like *King's Norton*, EH 419 i)
they cannot be called congregational.* His birth date is often

* Hymnody must not occupy too much space in this book: but for perfect examples of
Restoration miniatures, turn to *David's Harp* (EH 378) and *Tunbridge* (EH88), and

given as 1670: Dearnley puts it no earlier than 1673. His death, by his own hand, took place in 1707. He was most gifted as a miniaturist.

Benjamin Rogers, the erratic organist of Magdalen College, Oxford, and composer of the well-known 'Magdelen Tower Hymn' (itself a nice piece of writing in this style: see EH 328) was another able minor composer of the time. So was John Weldon (1676–1736). William Croft (1678–1727) is more substantial, but in his work—'O Lord rebuke me not', *TECM* III p. 124 is typical—there is a touch of that tendency to be decorative but key-tied which was to become a besetting sin of writers in this style. 'God is gone up' (*TECM* III p. 140) is livelier in that it uses a change of rhythm for one of the 'verses' and plays about with Purcellian figures: but in the end the same applies to it. It is now credibly said that it was his setting of Psalm 130, performed in St Paul's Cathedral, that was one of the factors contributing on that historic day to what John Wesley refers to as his conversion.

Maurice Greene, among the younger contemporaries of Handel (1695–1755) rates as a major church musician of this period; John Travers (1703–58) perhaps hardly so, even if there is a certain rumbustious bonhomie in his 'Ascribe unto the Lord' (TCM 184). William Boyce (1710–79), best known as an editor and collector, had a noticeable original talent. But if one stands away from most of this later music one begins to see rhetoric increasing and a sense of vital musical structure receding. I cannot think that it is altogether prejudice that makes me feel that, for proportion and musical vitality, the hymn tune *Magdalen College* of William Hayes (EH 457)—a masterpiece in miniature if ever there was one—has as much real music in it as twenty pages of his own or most others' longer choral works.

Is Handel a contributor to English church music or not? According to *TECM,* not: and actually the amount of his music that can be sung in church services is fairly small. Nor is it, on the whole, his most characteristic or interesting music. (If one does hear him in church, one is almost certain to be getting a piece from an oratorio, or, on a very big occasion, a Chandos Anthem.)

---

note especially the melodic interval at the end of phrase 3 of the first, and the harmony in phrase 3 of the second.

But Handel clearly cannot go unmentioned, though in a sense it is to the next chapter that he is more relevant, since in church music he was not so much a leading composer as an influence; we shall have to commit ourselves to the unpopular judgment that he was a hardly less baneful influence than Mendelssohn, being so massively misunderstood by church composers. But here we can say that it was obviously Handel's special genius to be able to say, musically, the simplest things in a manner which was large-scale without ever being disproportioned. The least subtle of all great composers, this special gift of his is as subtle as anything we should attribute to the (at this time) still unknown Bach. Never did any composer make the achieving of tremendous effects seem so simple a process. Never was a composer so calamitously *imitable*.

But the effects of this are still ahead of us. In his lifetime Handel fitted beautifully into the English musical scene because it was precisely a sense of occasion that was the chief attribute of English society since Charles II's day. It is not uninteresting to notice in *TECM* the texts which are set by the composers who are represented in that third volume presumably as offering the best and most characteristic examples of their style. After the introductory Lawes miniatures, the most natural text for a composer in the dark days of puritan repression was that which William Child did set—'O Lord God, the heathen are come into thine inheritance'. Of twenty texts set in the ensuing pieces, two are liturgical canticle-sets, two are funeral sentences, and of the rest at most two can be called anything but confident and jubilant. If ever there was an illustration of what Basil Willey unforgettably called 'cosmic toryism' it is in this post-Restoration music. The circles in which it was sung were contented and secure and brilliant.

Other circles were not so. Quite apart from the miserable condition of the eighteenth-century poor and the eighteenth-century sick (not to mention the eighteenth-century offenders against the law), that of the eighteenth-century parish outside metropolitan centres was, by contrast with higher circles, grey and spiritless. It was usually sufficient for a congregation at worship in the ordinary parish church to be content with a service almost all of which was read, and with a metrical psalm or two sung to one of the half-dozen tunes they knew. The later barrel-organ repertory of twenty or twenty-four tunes was considered as ample, indeed as far beyond the specific needs of any one congregation, as the repertory of a hymnal with 600 hymns is thought to be now. 'In quires and places where they sing', said the 1662 Prayer Book (1549 and 1552 didn't say even that) 'here followeth the Anthem'. This was the only concession* to music-making in the whole of that book, was a provision for precisely those royal chapels and other major music-making centres which the new authorities wanted, in the teeth of puritan protest, to promote. What happened out in the country, nobody cared very much.

It is fair to ask, then, why the first half of the century proves to be the source for so much hymnody which we now approve and know well. The answer must be that although many new psalters, celebrating in this miniature form the riches of the new music, were published between 1677 and 1740, almost all of them had no more than what we should now think of as private circulation. John Bishop published in 1711 an edition of Isaac Watts's hymns with music—not, of course, a tune for every hymn in the modern way of hymnals, but with a tune at least for every metre and a good selection of 'common tunes' for use with the great majority which were in C.M. It may have been looked at in Watts's church and a few others, but as we now say it never 'got off the ground'. The only such music source with any hope of circulation was the *Supplement* (1708) to the *New Version* of the Psalms (Tate and Brady), which produced a very good, and very up-to-date, selection of tunes to go with the new Psalter. Two of these are those we now know in England to 'Our God, our help in ages past' and 'O worship the King.' But even this did not get very far, since the *New Version*, very well received among American Episcopals, was not greeted with enthusiasm in its own country. The great repertory of early eighteenth-century music, choral and congregational, that we now have is the result of the researches of nineteenth-century and twentieth-century scholars who have revived, especially in hymnals, what was forgotten quite soon after its original appearance.

---

* The inclusion of Cosin's *Veni Creator* in the rite of Ordination is not an exception to this. It was designed to be read responsively or solo. (Any mathematician can discern that it does not really fit the plainsong tune now always associated with it.)

One form of music which seems to have appeared first during this time was the anglican chant. This was the very natural product of the impact of metrical and harmonized music on Gregorian plainsong, and what at first sight seems strange is that it was so slow to appear. If anglican chant is a very short hymn tune with a flexible reciting note to accommodate the varying lengths of verses in the English prayer-book psalter, then it would have found some sort of a market from 1549 onwards. The reason for its slow appearance is that where prose psalms were sung (and this was almost entirely in cathedrals and collegiate churches) the new polyphony made terms with Gregorian chant by providing fa-burden as an acceptable choral elaboration; and plenty of examples of this are available, although they seem to be confined to only a handful of the forty possible Gregorian chants in the Sarum use. William Byrd has a solitary example prefiguring free-composed anglican chant in his 5-part setting for Psalm 114 (to be found in *Oxford Chant Book* no. 2 in a 4-part reduction), but apart from this anglican chant as we know it, with its melody in the treble, setting two verses rather than one (that is, double rather than single) does not seem to be traceable before 1700. The two pioneers are usually quoted as 'Robinson in E flat' (this antiquated and unserviceable form of reference is still used: why doesn't somebody catalogue them under names of Old Testament characters?), dated 1706, and 'Flintoft in G minor', dated 1727. The second of these is an arrangement of a psalm tune (metrical) in Allison's 1599 *Psalter*. A few single chants may be earlier than 1700, but some that purport to be are later arrangements from phrases in works by composers who would be surprised at what has been done with them.

Anglican chant, it is usually now agreed, is choral rather than congregational music in essence, although it established itself in parishes very firmly during the nineteenth century. As congregationally performed, it tended always to make a curious sound which could not commend itself to sensitive ears, chiefly because of the distortions of rhythm to which unskilled singers were tempted under the pressure of a nervous doubt about how fast they should sing the reciting note. In consequence the form has been more heavily disparaged than it ought to have been; for, given sensitive performance and the avoidance of those musical vices to which chants, like hymn tunes, became specially vulnerable, it provides an excellent contemplative exercise in the interpretation and assimilation of psalmody both for those who hear and for those who (as is proper) listen.

Congregational music, however, received a powerful impulse in quite new directions from the Evangelical Movement, to which we are about to turn. In Restoration times the growing-points of music were still always in the choral styles. This Restoration period is ample in output, limited in terms of significant music; but in modern times, when resources and sympathies are alike broader than they were, we can hear a Restoration verse anthem in all its sumptuousness, string orchestra, trumpets, professional soloists and all, and the sense of space and opulence this always gives reminds us that the Restoration period placed its public emphases precisely on space and opulence. This kind of music is at its best when it can spread itself and when its composer has the strength to control the new rhetorical forces it uses. Let the composer's concentration flag, or the resources become defective, and it begins to sound trivial and platitudinous. The worst mischief was done when the Church found that it did not mind too much if this was what it was.

4. THE EVANGELICAL AGE, 1738–1847

This is the point at which we have to abandon our tidy and convenient pattern of dating our chapters in accordance with the sections of church music history implied in the *Treasury of English Church Music*. I have set the terminal dates as that of the 'conversion' of John Wesley and that of the publication of Havergal's *Old Church Psalmody* (of which more later) and of the death of Crotch.

Looked at from the point of view of the historian of cathedral music, this is, heaven knows, a barren period. Kenneth Long, in his magnificent and ample account* devotes eight of 480 pages to the period and mentions four composers, Jonathan Battishill (1738–1801), Thomas Attwood (1765–1838), Samuel Wesley (1766–1837) and William Crotch (1775–1847). *TECM* Volume IV adds to these Benjamin Cooke (1734–93) and Samuel Arnold (1740–1802) as composers of music worth recording as examples.

Of these six, a generous use of the word 'distinguished' would embrace Battishill, Wesley, and conceivably Attwood. It is worth glancing at the Cooke Magnificat (*TECM* IV p. 1) and the Arnold *Nunc Dimittis in A* (p. 18) merely for the purpose of seeing how commonplace music could get: it is hard to deny that all the sparkle, the mischief and the profundity of the Restoration composers seems to have given way to a sombre clerical platitudinousness; and the fact is that the music of such composers as those two is the cathedral's concession to the music of evangelical cliché. Beneath it there is a very considerable underworld of long-forgotten key-tied homophonic single-style music whose only purpose is to get the Evensong Canticles economically sung and fill up a defective service-list.

The two outstanding figures are, of course, Battishill and the elder Wesley. Battishill is best known, and rightly, for his sumptuous setting of the text 'O Lord, look down from heaven' (*TECM* IV p. 9). The whole piece is full of densely-contrived music, but the really remarkable thing about it is its composer's exercise of imagination. He was brought up as a chorister in Wren's St Paul's, and he imagines himself there as he is composing his setting: exploiting the legendary echo with long periods of musical

* *The music of the English Church,* Hodder & Stoughton, 1972.

silence—used with consummate skill at the great climax, bars
75–87, in which there are four half-bar silences for the whole
choir, and two whole-bar silences; this dramatic effect, reinforced
with ruthless chromaticisms, is contrasted with a flowing counterpoint, with beautifully timed voice-entries, in the rest of the piece.
This is a classic of any age; and 'Call to remembrance' is hardly
less so.

But, for Battishill, that may be, for the present age, about all.
When we come to Samuel Wesley, the younger son of Charles the
hymn writer and father of Samuel Sebastian, we come to one of
the great eccentrics in a field mostly populated by very conven-
tional characters. I have elsewhere argued that his largest personal problem was being the son of Charles;[*] certainly in his way
of life he was a dissenter against most established values—as was,
in different ways, his elder brother, Charles Junior (1757–1834).
A glance at *Exultate Deo* (*TECM* IV p. 29) and its companion piece
(not written at the same time) *In exitu Israel* shows that we are here
dealing with a musician whom anyone must take seriously.
Perhaps, by a short head, *Exultate,* with its absolutely continuous
energy and sure-footed stride, is the greater piece, but there is not
much between them. But this is not strictly English church music:
it is music written under the influence of that very interesting
pocket of Roman Catholic culture, the Chapel of the Portuguese
Embassy in London. Samuel in his early years frequented the
place for the sufficient reason that you were likely to get a better
musical diet there than anywhere else in London. True, it was
more likely to be imported Catholic music than English; but in
the 1780s the music programme there was lively and at least
would not expose any listener to *Arnold in A*.[†] But Samuel, unlike
his almost equally eccentric son, is hardly a figure in English
church music except in the broadest sense. He fulfilled only fitfully the bright promise of his early music as a composer: and he
is best respected for his tireless work in making the then unknown
J. S. Bach known in England.

[*] *The Musical Wesleys* & Jenkins, 1969).

[†] Obviously the place attracted plenty of people who were not Catholics (the Roman
Catholic faith being, of course, still legally prohibited in England). The tune we know to
'O come, all ye faithful' was sung there to that hymn in Latin, Protestant editors within a
few years were putting it into their tune-books, to hymns like 'Begone, unbelief', and
calling it *PORTUGUESE TUNE*).

Attwood is affectionately remembered for one or two miniatures. 'Come, Holy Ghost' is a melody of which Mozart could have been proud—perfect in its way, but its scale is that of the hymn tune; indeed it must be one of the earliest of those 'hymn-anthems' which later became so popular—being pieces in the hymn style so arranged as to sound best when sung by a choir. 'Turn thy face from my sins' is hardly greater in scope, and perhaps less captivating in execution.

As for Crotch—the famous (I am tempted to say notorious) 'Lo, star-led chiefs' is a monument of comic Handel. It really cannot be called much more. On paper it looks innocent enough—entertaining accompaniment, a naif picture of the Wise Men marching (if that's what they did) to the Manger. But to the ear the incessant thump of the root-position G major chord, the key-tied impression (like an able but uninspired improvisation) that one gets throughout the length of this is only made more exasperating by the one modulatory excursion at bars 36–42 which is hardly better than crude, which is hastily abandoned, and which is then, to the listener's horror, repeated. This was the musician who thought the hymn tune *St Michael*• a tolerable paraphrase of the 101st Genevan psalm tune. Like the two musical sons of Charles Wesley he was probably ruined by being noticed as a child prodigy. 'Lo, star-led chiefs' is part of an oratorio, *Palestine* (1812) and represents therefore part of a new English attempt to shine in a form to which Handel had given life.

Now it must be obvious that this is not all there is to say about the period we are here discussing. Three cathedral pieces of un-assailable magnificence cannot be the whole musical story. Of course it is not; but music-making has, for the time being, passed into the hands of people who have nothing to do with the high culture of anglicanism: the evangelicals.

The period of the Wesleyan campaign to re-Christianize Britain (it was nothing less) is externally notable—for I pass over the theological and spiritual aspects of it altogether—for a concerted and efficient rebellion against the social complacency of the age. It has been shown over and over again by historians that if you

---

• EH 27, AM 142 and everywhere else.

name a movement of social reform—the education of the poor, the improvement of prisons, the change of attitude towards the sick and the mentally handicapped, the abolition of slavery, there is an evangelical behind it. The missionary explosion of 1792 and the following years is part of this. The preaching and administrative ability of John Wesley and his staff when combined with the dawning romantic movement led people to seek adventure and fulfilment in the direct service of their fellows—especially their less privileged fellows. With all the lofty spiritual emphasis of the Wesleyan revival, expressed in the greatest of Charles Wesley's hymns, there went a thoroughly down-to-earth impulse to make this country a better place. Wesley's genius was in his ability to attract to his projects people of great influence and of widely differing temperaments. Never forget that the two greatest Wesleys lived and died anglican priests. They were not in any technical sense nonconformists; they profoundly dissented from the complacency which misapplied calvinism could induce in the successful, and they offered the Gospel to the unsuccessful in a manner which at first alarmed the Establishment.

There were two ways in which this affected the story of church music. The most obvious of these is hymnody. The Wesleys delivered everybody (as Isaac Watts had delivered the people of his own communion) from the tyranny of the metrical psalm. Watts taught his congregations to sing about Christ; the Wesleys taught the whole country to do so. Music was required for this, and Wesley knew where to find good professional musicians (like J. F. Lampe, 1703–51) to provide it. Hymnody is church music for the ordinary man, not to listen to, but to perform; and it seems to have been a principle of the early evangelicals that psalmody, admirable though its tunes so often were, underrated the ordinary man's appreciation of music and capacities for performance. Certainly in the new hymnody a new force in musical influence manifested itself powerfully: the English comic opera. There is plenty to be found in common between the texture of Pepusch's tunes in the *Beggar's Opera* and that of early Methodist tunes; but others of them have an *aria*-like melodic freedom which owes something to the pietist hymnody of Germany—from which country Lampe was an immigrant and to whose religion both the Wesleys owed so much in the maturing of their own. (It must be remembered that the way of life called since 1670 pietist had two foci: personal fervour and active participation in good works). Such a melody as that below has much of the flavour of one of those songs in the Schemelli *Gesangbuch* which J. S. Bach edited and harmonized.

J. F. Lampe
Hymns on the Great Festivals (1746) #10

The other way in which evangelical church music developed was through the great charity foundations which the teaching of the Wesleys inspired people to found. In London there were the Foundling Hospital, an orphanage, and the Magdalen and Lock Hospitals, the second of which was described as an institution 'for the restoration of unhappy females' (the Magdalen being for the same purpose). These three happen to have a connection with hymnody since all had their own hymn books.*

But it was the Lock which had the most influence. The site of this institution is now known as 18–20 Grosvenor Place, London. Its master was the celebrated Martin Madan (1726–90), whose experiences in administering the place led him to write a surprising book, *Thelyphthora* ('The Destruction of Women') that argued that polygamy would be a tolerable solution for the problem of prostitution. (Samuel Wesley was impressed by it at a time when his own domestic affairs were in some disorder: that story can be read elsewhere.) Under Madan, before that book

---

* See *EH* 69 ii for a tune from *Magdalen Hymns,* and 631 and 535 Pt 1 for tests from two different editions of the *Foundling Hospital Collection.*

obliged him to resign, the Lock, with its captive choir, became almost a nonconformist cathedral foundation in its promotion of singing and of new music. Of all the music in the *Lock Hospital Collection* (edited by Madan, 1769) only the fine hymn tune *Carlisle* (EH 190) is now remembered. But in its time the place made a great contribution. Anthems of a kind were certainly sung there, though they were always regarded as a kind of hymn. If we quote the melody line of *Denmark,* from that Collection, it will show what Madan thought choral music was. It is something like a verse anthem, although there is no independent continuo bass, and it owes something to Handel's diction. This is a setting of 'Before Jehovah's awful throne':

to — thy Name? We'll crowd thy gates with thank - ful —
songs, high as the heav'ns our voi - ces — raise; and earth, and
earth with her — ten thou - sand thou - sand tongues shall fill thy
courts with soun - ding — praise: shall fill thy courts with soun - ding —
praise, shall fill shall fill thy courts with soun - ding praise. (praise.)
Wide, wide as the world is thy com - mand, vast as e - ter - ni - ty, e-
- ter - ni - ty thy love; form as a — rock — thy truth — must — stand when
rol - ling — years shall cease to — move, — shall cease to move, when rol - ling —
years shall cease to — move, when rol - ling years — shall cease to move.

Lock Hospital Collection, 1769, page 94; verse 3 marked
as added by "W. Dixon", scored for treble and bass;
the remained scored in 3 parts + treble, tenor and
figured bass. Expression marks as in 1769 source except
those in v 3 which are from Rippon's *Collection*, c. 1796.

The impression one gets from studying this and similar books
is that choral singing was to this culture something very different
from what it was in a cathedral. The choir was, as it were (I do not
mean physically) nearer to the congregation. The kind of tune
that most people regard as 'characteristically Methodist' is the
tune which, once it has got launched, breaks into a sort of
primitive polyphony with an imitative *fugato* towards the end. The
less developed form of this is in the expansion of the tune towards
the end, requiring repetitions of words, of which a very beautiful
example is *Helmsley* ('Lo, he comes'), and an even more familiar

one, from an alien source we have mentioned before but originally written by an English hand, 'O come, all ye faithful'. This device of *fugato* (rather than that of straight repetition) seems to have accompanied manifestations of protestant praise much earlier in Scotland, where as early as 1625 we have 'fuguing tunes' in the Aberdeen Psalter of that year (consult the 1929 *Scottish Psalter* for two of these). This kind of behaviour is, as it were, treating a congregation like a choir; and this bringing together of two musical units which in the anglican tradition were so firmly kept apart was typical of the way these evangelicals conducted their churchmanship.

A lot of this was massively healthy and cheerful. But of course it led to triviality, and to the acceleration of that degeneracy which we mentioned in the previous chapter—abundant rhetoric, precious little reason. But another and very significant thing was happening to music when it got into the hands of people who were more zealous than scrupulous. This—and the process went on more or less unchecked until 1900—was the assimilation to the contemporary style of music written in other traditions and other musical vocabularies.

The reader may care to look at the two following examples: the first is from a collection edited by George Whitefield in about 1753, the other from the *Lock Hospital Book* of 1769:

It is possible to recognize the *Passion Chorale* behind the second, but the presence of *Tallis's Canon* behind the first is perhaps more elusive. And the interesting thing is that (although this by no means always happened in such transformations) the new version is in itself a very pleasant piece. *Brentwood* was certainly very popular in the second half of the eighteenth century: it keeps on turning up in successive hymnals.

Now this is something quite new, and something of which one never hears in histories of cathedral music, except perhaps when

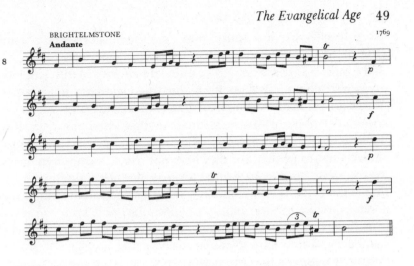

BRIGHTELMSTONE   1769
Andante

8

their authors cast a frowning glance at inept Victorian editions of Tudor anthems. It is the appearance in church music of a phenomenon which is appropriate to folk music. For if folk music is essentially music that does not depend on a written record for its transmission, then such music is always vulnerable to the defects of memory, the personal whims of the transmitter, and, in the end, the way singers insist on singing it. It has no 'true text', and such music, when it is written down, may well appear in many different forms. To take only one example: Benjamin Britten's folk song arrangement 'The Star of County Down' is the same tune as the hymn tune *Kingsfold,* and nobody can say that one is the 'correct' version and the other 'incorrect'. The opposite is true of any piece which is always performed from a written text—and all the music we have so far considered has been of that sort.

But what we have here is the deliberate abandonment of a written text—or that is what it looks like. You have the transformation of *Tallis's Canon* from a piece of witty and persuasive polyphony (there never was a better canon) into a new-style hymn tune with a pleasant melody and an adequate bass; you have the *Passion Chorale* totally anglicized from a chorale into a solo. And then, at that point, you are pulled up sharp: for actually is this not exactly what Bach did, when forming the *Passion Chorale* we know, with the old hymn tune *Herzlich Thut Mich Erlangen* (1613) which itself was a 'baptizing' of a secular love-song, 'Mein G'Muth ist mir verwirret' (1601)?

We must not pause here to examine the morals of this, still less to prove* that what J. S. Bach did was legitimate while what others do may, in the hands of lesser musicians, turn out to be criminal. The point here to be made is that when music reaches down towards the unmusical who want to sing (and people in church tend to be that, for they have not come to church to listen to concerts), this may happen as soon as they begin singing music that is not actually contemporary. If such a community builds up a repertory of historic music, only scholars will keep the texts pure, and they will be able to do that only when they have persuaded the community to accept their findings.

Now it happens that the period 1900–50, a period so rapidly passing into history, was one in which the scholars made more headway than they had ever made in persuading ordinary singers to widen their vocabulary, get interested in historical faithfulness, and 'sing it right.' But in the period 1750–1900 that is not the kind of thing people were interested in. They lived, aesthetically, much more in the present. E. H. Fellowes memorably showed† in the last of those cathedral lists which he reprinted at the end of his *English Cathedral Music,* how as late as 1896 a cathedral repertory would be of music which was entirely written (or if older, edited) within not much more than fifty years of its performance there.

The prevailing idea among such communities, then, is that if anything is to be sung it must appear to have been written by Mr Handel or one of his disciples. Should its accent be of another age, that must be (in a disgusting word coined by a later anti-historical age) updated. What couldn't be updated was left where it was.

Now over against this we must say that the evangelicals did explosively increase the vocabulary of their congregations. These people did not have to get along on six metrical psalm tunes. The massive choirs—following the example of the captive choirs of the Hospitals—led the singing and everybody joined in

---

* I said a little about this in *The Music of Christian Hymnody* (1957)—which has long been out of print; I propose to develop the matter in a rewritten version later.

† I refer to the first edition; these were omitted (lamentably) in J. A. Westrup's recent revision. See p. 259 of the 1941 edition.

enthusiastically, carried along by the attractiveness of the music.

This is where we have to return to our proposition, made at the end of the last chapter, that Handel has much to answer for. This was in no sense his fault, and we do not say it as we would say it of Gounod in the nineteenth century. But Handel has that faculty for making massive statements simple, and simple ideas massive. It really did look to many composers as if anybody could write like Handel. Nobody really thought that about Mozart (though probably some, equally deluded, thought it about Haydn). One of the ways Handel makes his effects is by making a short text go a long way (as in the *Hallelujah Chorus,* to take a handy example, or as in the *Amen Chorus* at the end of that work, to take an extreme one). From this, many took the cue of simply repeating words until the music had caught up. In hymns this could occasionally work, when a stanza always ended with a similar line—like 'All hail the power of Jesus' name';* elsewhere of course it soon becomes preposterous. In anthems it is a practice which stayed with us right into the twentieth century—and then was rapidly abandoned. Except in acknowledged masterpieces like Battishill's 'O Lord, look down', where the repetitions are carefully contrived, it is on the whole as irritating to modern ears as polyphony, which obscured the words, was to the puritans. It is difficult to see why they objected to obscurity without equally fiercely objecting to the trivializing of texts through repetition, except if the answer be that repetition was, though not unknown, less evident when the puritans were at their fiercest. In people like Wesley and Whitefield, both of whom raised the old objection against polyphony repeatedly, the inconsistency is less excusable.

We do see in this age the beginning of that musical inflation which debased its currency. This is always a symptom of activist success, and it will always be a symptom in church music of evangelistic success. Band wagons will roll and people will jump on them.

If this is all very questionable so far as music goes, that is not the whole story. Evangelical success led to the formation of large congregations meeting in new, massive, buildings, often quite outside the field of the Established Church, and often, like the Surrey

* I refer to the English tune, *Miles Lane,* not the one used in America.

Chapel where Rowland Hill (1744–1833) was minister for nearly half a century, with better choirs and far more resourceful organs than were in the cathedrals, let alone the parish churches. But evangelical zeal always had its pedagogic side, and one consequence of all this was the rise of singing classes in the earlier nineteenth century, with the rapid spread of musical literacy among the hitherto musically uneducated. This was materially assisted by John Curwen when he first introduced the tonic sol-fa system of singing in 1842: and Curwen was a Congregationalist minister. John Pyke Hullah (1812–84) began his singing classes in Battersea in 1840, and these spread to many other centres during his lifetime. Henry James Gauntlett (1805–76) adapted the same technique to a Congregational church in Islington, and here and also at Carr's Lane, Birmingham, choir practice was a wholly congregational engagement, where people came (paying a fee) to learn not only Sunday's hymns, but Sunday's anthems as well. Later in the century hymnals of the Congregationalist and Baptist kind always provided, either as companion volumes or as part of the hymn-book, selections of from sixty to a hundred anthems in which everybody present was invited to join. This is taking us a little outside our present period but it was the direct consequence of the placing of church music in the hands of ordinary people. This de-professionalizing caused plenty of music to be written to a standard from which a cathedral organist, or any other sensitive musician, would turn away in horror; but for what it was, it was at least a natural and historically explicable development, and it went right back to the Lock Chapel.

In case anybody is tempted to think that all evangelicals and all nonconformists were activist philistines, it should be mentioned (we have no space here to develop the subject) that in certain parts of the nonconformist body, especially in Congregationalism, nineteenth-century thinkers were considering the fate of liturgy very seriously. Among these were Thomas Binney (1798–1874), a London minister of sensitive and poetic mind, who in the King's Weigh House was the first non-anglican minister to introduce the singing of psalms to anglican chants, in the 1830s, and John Spencer Curwen, son of the John Curwen mentioned above, who wrote some of the most penetrating criticisms of the customs of his co-religionists that that age allowed to see the light.

But yes—we have to admit that cathedral music and parish music in the still orthodox parts of the Church of England were in bad shape.

One of the most interesting sidelights on parish church music is provided in the late Canon Noel Boston's book, *Church and Chamber Barrel Organs.** The great age of these—replacing gallery bands—was the early nineteenth century: they were in existence before, mostly in private homes. As a monument of musical technology they had some appeal in an age which was getting used to machinery, and finding the recruitment of even barely tolerable musicians difficult. Country churches seem to have been glad of them. Canon Boston after much research compiled a list of the hymn tunes available on 63 of these instruments, which played from pre-set barrels and required only the turning of a handle to produce the sound. The 63 instruments produce a total of thirty different tunes, of which only the *Old Hundredth* and *Tallis's Canon* appear on all the machines. The reasonable deduction was that in the parishes thirty tunes was the total repertory; it looks likely that not more than a handful were what could be called universally familiar.

Mr John Wilson pointed out to me one curious piece of information that one gets if one activates one of these machines, which is that hymn singing must in those days have been astonishingly slow; a normal speed of turning the handle produces a speed in the music little better than half what even the English (one is tempted to say, a quarter of what the Americans) are now used to.

It cannot have been until the early 1840s that any serious attempt was made to enlarge the repertory. The most famous such attempts were Vincent Novello's *The Psalmist,* in four parts the last of which is dated 1843, and the *Union Tune Book,* of the same year. But the format of these and similar collections indicates that it was normal for the tune book and the hymnal to be separate books; only the choir (if there was one) and the precentor in a parish would have copies of the music: everybody else sang from a words-only book.

The stimulus to increase the vocabulary was a spin-off from evangelical hymnody, of course, and what new hymnody was

---

* Lindsay G. Langwill, Edinburgh, 1967.

produced in the first half of the nineteenth century was distinctly
of the evangelical flavour, free-ranging, tending to vulgarity or
when that was repressed, to dulness, and rarely producing
anything that later generations have found worth holding on to.
Anglican music was becalmed; most other people's was blown
about by mindless fashion. If one were asked to find half a dozen
fine hymn tunes from the period 1800–40 one might well have to
be content with Thomas Clark's *Warsaw*, William Horsley's
Belgrave, and possibly Turle's *Westminster*.* Methodism was
producing such terrifying offerings as *Sagina* (*c.* 1800) and *Diadem*
(*c.* 1840).† It was time something happened.

* EH 386, 511, 441 *Church Hymnary* (1927) 165, 26, 23.
† *Methodist Hymn Book* (1933) 371 i and Appendix 6.

5. THE NEW SERIOUSNESS, 1833–76

If the period covered in the last chapter gave the nonconformists and unorthodox anglicans a brief moment in the centre of the stage, the period 1847–99 thrusts them, so far as music goes, back into the wings. For this is the period which in English church music is dominated by two historic developments, the Oxford Movement and the general crusade for the improvement of church music. Before we mention the music, we must give some brief account of these.

The Oxford Movement ought, of course, to be called the London Movement, because it was mostly in the metropolis that things, in the first generation of that epoch, moved. But it began in Oxford, and is always dated from John Keble's Assize Sermon of 1833, delivered in St Mary's Church, Oxford, where John Henry Newman was vicar.

If one is to put very shortly a story which can easily be expanded to fill a fat volume, the Oxford Movement was the English Counter-Reformation, prompted by a growing conviction in the minds of its promoters that England must choose between going atheist and going Methodist. It must have looked like that to them. We have already mentioned the pervasive effects of evangelicalism; we can now add that although evangelicals in John Wesley's time were mostly anglicans who did not conform to the customs, social or disciplinary, of their church, it was not long after Wesley's death that Methodism formed itself into a dissenting denomination.* It had been regarded as such for long enough by orthodox anglicans. The question was whether the Church of England as by Law Established could ever be brought back to what they held to be its proper position of authority and respect.

---

* The intimacies of a complicated history do not really concern us here. Methodists date the founding of their Church from 1739, and indeed the word *Methodist* was coined in 1729 by John Wesley. Methodist Conference, their governing body, was first appointed in 1784 by the Founder. Probably the enactment of 1795 that the admission of a preacher to full connection with Conference conferred rights of ordination completed a breach which had certainly been widening since John Wesley's ordinations of ministers for America in 1784. Secessions from orthodox or Wesleyan Methodism speedily followed, but the union of certain smaller bodies in 1907, and the union of those with the Wesleyans in 1932 produced the Methodist Church as now known in Britain. For further details see appropriate reference books such as the *Oxford Dictionary of the Christian Church*.

The programme which formed the 'movement' had as its chief emphasis the rediscovery of the teachings, customs, liturgies and ethos of the pre-Reformation Church which had been discarded at the Reformation. Though the impulse was laudable, the practice of it was naturally enough inspired by romanticism—a new cult of the past which was especially celebrated in the novels of Sir Walter Scott. But romanticism would not have been enough, though without a touch of this the movement might never have got started. Scholarship—itself a strange enough activity to have a touch of heroic adventure about it for most parsons—had to come to its aid.

So among the products of the Oxford Movement some of the first were a new interest in the works of the early Christian Fathers, and the providing of new English editions of them, along with new explorations of the forms of worship enjoyed by the medieval church. It is these, of course, that concern us most, but we can mention also that the prompters of the Movement saw scholarship only as undergirding wholly practical measures to bring the Church of England back into the lives of people whom it had ignored for more than a century—the people of the parishes.

The Movement, in its principles and effects, looks like an anti-puritan movement. It is not quite correct so to describe it. In one sense it was a quest for excellence in a field where mediocrity had reigned, and that is a wholly puritan value. In another, it was concerned with re-evangelizing a country which had developed into something very different from those Middle Ages in which it found its inspiration, and its promoters on the whole showed a thoroughly puritan practicality in making the necessary adaptations of technique.

Much of their attention was given to a re-evaluation of the life and duties of the clergy. Strong gestures were made in favour of priestly celibacy, which did not in the end succeed, and the re-foundation of monastic communities was encouraged, which communities have been among the most powerful agents of inspiration in the Church of England ever since.

But concerning worship, the point they were making had consequences for church music which resulted in considerable tensions. I am writing nearly a century and a half after the inception of this movement, but some of these tensions are points of vigorous controversy at this very moment.

One can put it like this. The Tractarians (a useful one-word designation, derived from the *Tracts for the Times,* all written near the year 1836, in which their principles were basically stated) sought to revive the devotions of the medievals. This meant reviving the structure of worship as then understood, and especially the proper use of the Offices, and their clear distinction from the Eucharist. Now the only places where the Offices were publicly performed to any extent were the cathedrals, which were and are, of course, what remains of the medieval monastic foundations, and, possibly (though in 1833 fitfully) the college chapels of the ancient universities. What the parish church had was the anglican revision of the Offices which is Morning and Evening Prayer (1662 version); and this had come to be very much a preaching and teaching service. It was wrested from the true context of the Office, which is in medieval terms a service appropriate to a certain hour of every day, variable at certain high seasons, not a service to be used on Sunday as the common people's main diet of worship. The Tractarians wanted to put it back where it belonged, ‐‐ a support to the central service of the Eucharist, which from the beginning they wished to make (and which by the mid-twentieth century their successors had succeeded in making) the central act of worship on the Lord's Day. It was always every parson's duty to read his Office privately; but all Offices are so cast as to be ideally performable only in a community: they are always in the form of conversations, not of monologues. The ideal was to have, not only in every cathedral, but also in every parish, a community of the faithful, including a team of at least two priests, who would keep the Offices alive. In practice this did not, except in monastic communities, get further than the priest's at least taking the Prayer Book as it stood more seriously.

Now the high tradition of English church music is centred always on the cathedral, with its choir and its team of priests. That is why it is much easier to write this chapter (and much more difficult to write the previous one) if one's subject is only cathedral music. Cathedral music 'majors' in anthems and settings of the Canticles. The parish Eucharist according to the Tractarian view 'majors' in plainsong, with perhaps a concession here and there in the use of a choral Mass.

If one takes too narrow a view of the Oxford Movement, one will see it in the end as an anti-cathedral force, or at any rate as a kind of neo-Gregorian force for limiting the contribution music can make in church to what is appropriate to the Eucharist. And that would be understandable. It is one of the secrets of the aesthetic success of Evensong that its 'script', as it were, is light enough in weight to permit plenty of musical embellishment without a sense of disproportion. To be crudely practical, it is short enough in duration for elaborate musical settings not to make it too lengthy—and that is even more so when the 1662 ac-cretions before the Preces are omitted (as in choral evensong they really should be). It is otherwise with a parish Eucharist such as the Tractarians were hoping for (and got). This is a quite different act of worship; it contains in its 'script' a drama so profound and ultimate that it is quite easy for elaborate music to have a choking effect. This the Tractarians knew very well, and it was one of their main reasons for promoting plainsong.

Why then do we regard the Oxford Movement as a major force in the revival and refreshment of English Church Music? The answer is, because we are not merely concerned with the cathedral and because the movement itself was behind all its practical exhortations contemplative, patient, scholarly and serious-minded about the Church.

It was a pursuit of excellence, and as such its leaders knew what they should encourage at parish level. They encouraged the priest to be devoted and industrious, and a figure to earn the respect of the obscure as well as of the landed aristocracy. But then they en-couraged the parish choir to raise its morale (and vastly to im-prove its behaviour) by robing it in vestments familiar then only in cathedrals, and to do at least some of the things that cathedrals did, like singing the Responses instead of mumbling them. But as for the cathedrals, there can be no doubt that the new spirit was responsible for much that was done there to improve the working conditions, and the behaviour, of choristers and organists—a matter to which we are about to come.

Above all, this movement reinstated imagination as a legitimate factor in worship. Puritanism was always so explicit: the typical Wren church with its open plan and conspicuous

pulpit, caricatured in the older parish church which was adapted
to puritan style by the placing of a three-deck pulpit between the
people and the altar, is a monument to explicitness: the baroque
style is similarly a monument to overstatement. The Tractarian
revival of the Gothic style—which came in for much ribaldry in
the confident 1930s—was a recovery of imagination. However ill
it was done (and not seldom it was done superbly well) it imported into the parish something of what the cathedral stood for.

And we must remember what the parishes were. It was one
thing to reform worship in an already delicious medieval parish
church in East Anglia; it was another to provide a new church for
a parish which, in a new industrial town, was solid slums. In
England there is no better illustration of this than the sight of
St Bartholomew's, Brighton. Brighton, considered as a fashion-
able watering-place, was adequately served by a decent parish
church built by the architect who designed the Houses of
Parliament—the architecture of this is very mildly Gothic, and it
stands modestly remote from the old parish church that served
the original sailors and fishermen for hundreds of years. But if
you look down on the town from one of the hills over which it
now sprawls into suburbs, you do not see St Nicholas, the old
fishermen's church, or St Peter's, the demure parish church. You
see a huge building, uncompromisingly rectangular with a steep-
pitched roof atop, rising some eighty feet from the ground, sur-
rounded by (presumably now only the remains of) hundreds of
cottages whose elevation probably never exceeded eighteen. That
is St Bartholomew's, and it was built by people who knew that
Brighton was a place where railway engines were built—which in
the later nineteenth century it was. Now it is the brazen oppor-
tunism of this that shows the Oxford Movement at its most practical. *These* were people to whom something imparting a vast
'sense of occasion' would appeal; and the highly tractarian
worship within, with movement, lights, incense and a huge sense
of distance and excitement giving life to the deep devotion of the
faithful, was what there and in every industrial town the Tractarians provided. The churches are often ugly outside, over-
ornate within: but the simple mind gets the message that
something of enormous importance tends to go on there. This is
all done by giving freedom to that imagination which the puritan

mind always suspected. And if it be replied that this is to give free range to superstition, that charge must be fully admitted. Only those who can see as much essential beauty in a really 'vintage' puritan meeting house as in a Gothic church (or as in Wren's St Paul's) are really alive to the tensions which are always present in a field where so many forces are at work as that of religion.

Imagination, then, is the opening through which the Oxford Movement could have its effect on music; but music is obstinate, as we now know, and it never takes all its orders, or even all its encouragements, from the clergy. About the last person to do so was Samuel Sebastian Wesley, the only musician in history who in one lifetime was organist of four cathedrals and also of a large parish church (Leeds) which he helped to turn into a near-cathedral foundation.

S. S. Wesley is pivotal to this story, but he was not the only person concerned with the improvement of church music; we shall mention one or two others in a moment. But he has his natural place here. This eccentric and dedicated musician, head and shoulders above any other composer of his generation in church music, and in any company perhaps second only to Sterndale Bennett, was born in 1810, the issue of an irregular union between his father Samuel and the woman he lived with after deserting his wife. And the best commentary on the condition of English church music in what we are still obliged to call the upper reaches is in his tract, *A Few Words on Cathedral Music and the Musical System of the Church, with a Plan of Reform*, published in Leeds (where he was organist) and London, in 1849.* The 'Few words' amount to a book about half the size of the present one devoted to a systematic and passionate exposure of the meagre and miserable conditions prevailing in most cathedrals. From evidence he has collected he shows that (somewhat in the manner of the Elizabethan church) the anglican church is hardly less than a conspiracy to demoralize musicians and suffocate music. Near the end he demands salaries of £500 to £800 a year for cathedral organists (you could multiply that by ten to get comparable figures to-day), and proper conditions of work for choristers and adult choirmen. He has much to say about the organs on which

* Some account of the life and work of S. S. Wesley will be found in my book, *The Musical Wesleys* (1969).

organists are required to play.

In respect of this last matter, which has much to do with the development of English church music, we may refer the reader to W. L. Sumner's authoritative book *The Organ* (Macdonald, 1953) which makes it quite clear that what we now call a full pedal board was virtually unknown in Britain before the Great Exhibition of 1851. He says (p. 176). 'of thirty-three British abbeys and cathedrals at the time only two, those at Westminster and Hereford, had a few separate pedal pipes.' Now Wesley had been at Hereford just after the time (the first quarter of the century) about which Dr Sumner wrote, and he knew what even 'a few separate pedal pipes' could do. And it comes as something of a shock to the modern reader, who is accustomed to hearing the organ and nothing else in church, that this instrument, right up to the second half of the nineteenth century, was regarded as nothing more than a continuo instrument in church. The great verse anthems of the Restoration composers presupposed a string band; when this disappeared, or where it was frowned on, all one had was an organ with a pedal board, if it had one at all, comparable to what one finds nowadays on the electronics used in American restaurants. There is that splendid story of Sir George Smart, who had played at the coronations of William IV and Victoria (and was the composer of the admirable hymn tune, *Wiltshire*) being invited to try one of the continental organs at the Exhibition with a full pedal board, and replying that he had lived to be 75 without playing on a gridiron, and didn't propose to begin then (quoted in Summer, *loc. cit.*). Indeed, S. S. Wesley's well-known anthem, 'Blessed be the God and Father' (1835) and Walmisley's Magnificat and Nunc Dimittis in D minor (1855) are the first cathedral choral pieces to include an independent organ part.

But S. S. Wesley was leading from strength. Not only had he had plenty of experience—at 39 he was half way through his third major appointment—but he knew that others were working along the same lines. His own vicar, Walter Hook at Leeds (later Dean of Chichester) had appointed him with the express purpose of reviving church music in that parish church; and Hook was only a very moderate Tractarian. St Mark's College, Chelsea, founded in 1841 by the National Society (itself an evangelical association dedicated to the improvement of the education of the

poor) had become, since the appointment of Thomas Helmore as
Vice-Provost, a vigorous centre of church music promotion, and
had indeed imported the talent of John Hullah, the most
renowned of public singing teachers, to run its programme. In
1845 Dr Robert Druitt, a physician with Tractarian views, issued
his pamphlet, *A Popular Tract on Church Music, with Remarks on its
Moral and Political Importance,* and the following year he founded,
with two London clergymen, the Society for Promoting Church
Music. In 1839 the Cambridge Camden Society, a society for
publishing documents on church architecture, furnishing and
music, was founded by three undergraduates at Trinity, Cambridge: Benjamin Webb, Alexander Hope and J. M. Neale (later
famous as a hymn-translator). The tide was already running, and
S. S. Wesley took advantage of it. Frederick Helmore, the brother
of Thomas, was carving out a career as a travelling choirmaster,
and doing very much for the 1840s what Martin and Geoffrey
Shaw did for the 1920s—spreading the infection of enthusiasm
for good church music. The admirable Mrs Maria Hackett
(1783–1874), who constituted herself an unofficial inspector of
choir-schools in order to expose and eradicate the evil conditions
under which choirboys lived, was, and had been for a long
generation by 1849, the scourge of every procrastinating bishop
and dilatory dean: beginning at St Paul's, London in 1811, for a
long time she visited every cathedral in the country (there were 33
at that time) once every three years; she had made a considerable
impression with her *Brief account of Cathedral and Collegiate Schools*
(1827), but she was still on her travels in the 1860s, and, however
much she terrified archdeacons and chancellors, she became
known as 'The Choristers' Friend'.

With all these voices raised against the degeneracy of music in
churches and cathedrals, with the 'new deal for organ builders'
that followed the exhibition of so many organs by continental
builders at the Great Exhibition of 1851, morale began to rise.
Only a year or two after Wesley's publication, The Reverend Sir
Frederick Ouseley (1825–89) was campaigning for the foundation
of St Michael's, Tenbury, which has been a centre of contemplative scholarship in church music since its opening in 1856.*

* The whole story which is here summarized is told in detail in Bernarr Rainbow's admirable book, *The Choral Revival in the Anglican Church, 1839–72* (Barrie & Jenkins, 1970).

To complete the picture, we may mention the attention which the Oxford Movement was drawing to itself. The controversy, and even rioting, which attended the foundation of St Barnabas, Pimlico (London)—a very characteristic example of the new anglo-catholic foundations in depressed areas which was consecrated in 1850, is typical of what could happen, when those very people whom the Church sought to evangelize were persuaded by journalists and politicians to raise their voices against the alleged popish pretensions of the new anglicanism. The establishment in that same year, 1850, of the Roman Catholic hierarchy under Bishop (later Cardinal) Wiseman was another occasion for anti-Catholic propaganda and demonstration. But persecution, where it is not too efficient, generates energy, and in certain places also sanctity, and the pressures put upon the anglo-catholics served only to sharpen their faculties, made it necessary for them to think and argue less romantically, and press on with their work, especially that among the poor. One could cite J. M. Neale, the liturgical scholar, hymn translator and writer of carols, as a victim of persecution to the extent that he was, though ordained, never licensed to preach in parishes, and had to spend his life as Warden of Sackville College at East Grinstead, which was a home for indigent elderly men.

It has to be said, in sum, then, that the Oxford Movement is part of what amounts to the English Counter-Reformation, and that it was the Church of England's good fortune that just about the middle of the century the forces of high scholarship formed a confluence with those of reforming zeal. So much, one has to say, was going on, after a period of unexampled apathy. Whatever one's religious sympathies, there was enough in this reformation to command one's respect: it was aesthetic, theological, social and practical; it was directed to the cultivated and the simple, the rich and the poor. It was at least a brave attempt to answer Wesley.

Since the whole project was so many-sided, its musical effects were felt at many levels, and these we must consider separately in considering the second half of the century: at the level of the cathedral, the parish, and the scholar.

6. THE CHURCH TRIUMPHANT AND TRIVIAL, 1851–99

The effects of the new thinking of the Oxford Movement were least marked, and slowest in being implemented, in the cathedrals. The stock of nineteenth-century cathedral music is not, on the whole, an encouraging sight. As we have said, it was the parishes on which the reformers trained their guns most of the time.

In cathedral music the one figure who towers over the rest is S. S. Wesley. Even during the period when reaction against nineteenth-century music was at its height in England the name of Wesley obstinately holds its place in cathedral lists. Nobody could ignore 'Thou wilt keep him in perfect peace', nor, for all its imperfections, could 'Blessed be the God and Father' be extricated from the affections of choirs and congregations.* Wesley, of whom enough has been written elsewhere to allow us to treat him quite briefly, was a visionary composer. He began writing when the reforms of church music had begun, but when their effects were mostly in the future. He wrote in a humane and red-blooded style, as one who knew more music by other composers, sacred and secular, than any of his contemporaries did. Some of his best works are lengthy, yet not on a scale to engage the attention of an oratorio choir. Therefore they are not heard as often as they might be. Such is *The Wilderness*, which is a verse anthem on an enormous scale. Like 'Blessed be the God and Father', another verse anthem, it uses an organ instead of a string orchestra. The *Service in E* is one of the longest, in matter of duration, in the whole repertory, and it contains many points of musical genius. So do the shorter anthems, 'Cast me not away' and 'Wash me throughly' (*TECM* IV pp. 81, 94).

But when you have mentioned Wesley, that solitary and, among his contemporaries, unpopular musician, who else is there? A glance at the contents of *TECM* IV that refer to this period gives the answer. Aside from Wesley, that collection offers eleven pieces by eight composers, and of those eleven, four are taken from works written on oratorio scale.

* *TECM* iv pp. 89, 73 : also at CAB Nos. 91 and 8. The selection of Wesley in CAB provides an excellent introduction to his work.

64

The rise of Victorian oratorio reflects the situation. It was in improving the environment of music, not in improving music itself, that the Victorians excelled. The organs were getting better, the choirs more cheerful, the singing classes were flourishing, and far more people wanted to sing. The church (and this applied outside the Church of England even more than inside it) was becoming a centre of music-making, and people joined choirs in the new large nonconformist foundations simply for the pleasure of singing. The way was being paved for the foundation of large occasional choirs in London and the provinces some of which became as famous as the Huddersfield Choral Society and the Oxford Bach Choir. All this was admirable, and it created a demand for large-scale music which the composers of oratorio were happy to satisfy. But naturally enough the demand could not create talent: it could create only willingness.

The example of John Stainer (1840–1901), one of the archetypal Victorians, is typical. Nothing could have been more beneficial than his influence on music-making: few influences have been more disastrous than that of his compositions. The one example of his work in *TECM* IV (p. 147) is the famous 'God so loved the world' from *The Crucifixion:* a blameless piece in itself extracted from a cantata (or oratorio: it is difficult to know how to categorize works of this sort) much of the rest of whose music, and the whole of whose libretto where it is not quoting scripture, is a caricature of the sensational triviality which, no matter how great the efforts of their latter-day defenders, we are bound to attribute to the Victorians. From *The Crucifixion* you go downwards into the underworld of Michael Costa, Caleb Simper and J. H. Maunder (the last two of whom prompted Vaughan Williams once to enliven one of his pugnacious comments about all this with the phrase 'composers with ridiculous names': their names are about the one thing these composers couldn't help; other aspects of their activities are less innocent).

TECM IV quite properly does not mention Stainer's *The Daughter of Jairus;* and that baneful work, Spohr's *The Last Judgment,* which amounts to the most trivial treatment conceivable of the immensities of the Book of Revelation, is, though it has enjoyed such popularity in England, happily outside their brief (and ours). Arthur Sullivan gets a few pages in *TECM* IV (p. 155) with a piece from 'The Light of the World'; another very well-known anthem of his used to be 'O Gladsome Light' from *The Golden Legend*, which is often to be found in those nonconformist congregational anthem collections we referred to earlier. Both of these have a 'Lost Chord' stickiness of melody and harmony which prompts some reflections on the way in which the genius of England's finest melodist, who was in his youth so profoundly influenced by Schubert, was deliberately suffocated when he wrote for the Church.

Of the offerings in *TECM* IV, only Goss's *If we believe,* Walmisley's Evening Canticles in D minor, and Ouseley's two motets 'Is it nothing to you?' and 'O Saviour of the world' seem to be of more than historical interest. Even Sterndale Bennett, who had so much to say elsewhere in music, hardly does himself justice in the opening phrases of 'God is a Spirit'. 'O that I knew where I might find him' (*CAB* 74) has, in its first half, much better music (near the end it lapses into platitude).

On the whole the Victorians are better, the smaller the forms they write in—as we are about to suggest. It was the immense activity created by the musical reforms, together with the enterprise of the house of Novello, founded in 1811, in beginning its inextinguishable Octavo series in 1846, that made music vulnerable to qualitative inflation. People demanded what they would enjoy, and the greater the multitude demanding, the narrower the band of accepted taste became. Indeed it was the very success of the reformation, together with the economic success of the churches themselves, that called forth so much second-rate music. The most dangerous demand in any artistic field is a popular demand for 'More of the same: as much as you can produce'.

So church music in the Victorian era tended to suffer from one of two distortions—a piece of any considerable length might well make room for both. One was simply the beating out thin of an inadequate musical idea, of which the external consequence was plain dulness. It is not difficult for a facile musician to bluff his way through on a very small store of musical wit, and that is why there are so many pages of plain dull and platitudinous music to be found here, just as there are near the end of the previous century. On the whole this is what one gets from Smart and Steggall—worthy composers in their way, but quite incapable of

sustaining a listener's interest for more than a page or two. One
besetting vice was properly pointed out by Fellowes* who showed
how addicted these composers were to a four-bar unit, and how
insensitive this made them to the values of words. But the other
quality of disproportion for which most of them are more
celebrated was in the lack of balance between rhetoric and reason
which, now that the vocabulary had been so much enriched by the
work of the great Viennese composers, as well as by a new
knowledge of the works of J. S. Bach, place at the disposal of any
half-baked composer an armoury of emotional weapons which
he was free to use whether or not he was capable of directing
them, or of using them as precision tools. On the whole it is
probably most serviceable to confine ourselves to one primary
example, in which will be seen a good variety of Victorian vices,
and whose quotation, because it is probably now quite unknown,
will give offence to nobody.

* English Cathedral Music, p. 215.

The composer of this piece is Myles Birket Foster (1851–1922), who was trained at the Royal Academy of Music under Sullivan and Ebenezer Prout, and who held organists' posts at various London churches, ending up at St Alban's, Holborn; he was an examiner for Trinity College, London, and worked as an editor for Boosey, the music publisher—a thoroughly respectable professional life.

I find this piece in the anthem section of the *Congregational Church* Hymnal (1887)—Anthem No. 57, and it turns out to be a setting of the third of the 'Great Os of Advent', a series of sentences appropriate to certain medieval Advent liturgies which had been rediscovered by the Tractarian liturgists (see EH 734).*
Without labouring the point unduly, we may draw the reader's attention to the following points:

(a) In 22 bars there are thirteen indications of expression in letters and, in the organ part, four pairs of crescendo-decrescendo wedges; also one isolated crescendo.

(b) In the voice part there are eight 'circumflex' accent marks and three arrowhead accents.

(c) The following 'stage directions' appear: (bar 1) *Andante religioso;* (bars 6 and 9) *'F ten p'* and *'F ten pp';* (bar 15) *sf;* (bar 18) *rall: dolce;* (bar 20) *Piu lento;* (bar 22) *ten.*

Beyond this, attend to the harmonic progression at bars 11–14, in which a promised modulation turns out to be a mirage, and to the extraordinary number of accented discords.

This is a beautiful example of music which contains nothing that a professor of harmony could possibly object to, and nothing which a musician can conceivably commend. Observe how necessary the composer finds it to supplement his voice parts with filled-out organ chords, and to add optional extra notes to the last three bars of the tenor and bass parts. Rhetoric of the most oleaginous kind replaces reason in this piece, and you can find any number of parallel examples in the underworld of Victorian church music. No more needs to be said about this.

---

* Liturgical scholars will find this an interesting byway to explore: the *Congregational Church Hymnal* was a very literate collection indeed so far as texts went, both of hymns and anthems, and it includes in its Anthem section what looks like the whole series of the Great Advent Os; but what actually happens is that Nos. 1–7 (down to *O Emmanuel*) are there as anthems 55–61, but the editors balk at *O Virgo Virginum* and substitute a text of similar form, 'O Holy of Holies', followed by another, 'O Shepherd of Israel', making a series of nine in all. While we are about it we may also mention the remarkable prose canticle, 'O Saviour of the world, the Son, Lord Jesus' (Chant No. 16), which first appears in this book, and is probably the one really significant contribution to liturgical texts made by this denomination.

Hymnody and the parishes

In the last few paragraphs we happen to have mentioned Henry Smart (1813–79), Charles Steggall (1826–93) and Myles B. Foster. There might be a case for saying that they are the composers of three of the best hymn tunes written in Victorian times: respectively, *Regent Square* (EH 431, AM 279), *Christ Church* (EH 411, AM 280), and *Crucis Victoria* (AM 306)*. For the story of church music it is fortunate indeed that the anglican hymn was virtually invented in the nineteenth century, because it is here that the Victorian composers show their best qualities. Much fun is poked at Victorian hymnody; but that is because this is the church music most people know best. A fairer judgment must deliver the verdict that in this miniature musical form these composers really did, at their best, know what they were doing.

The centre-piece in Victorian hymnody is inevitably *Hymns Ancient and Modern,* that fantastically successful hymnal which became a legend as no other hymnal in the world ever did. This book came from the Tractarian movement through the humanizing filter of the country parsonage. It was edited by a group of enthusiasts who set themselves to produce a hymn-book which would be a companion to the Book of Common Prayer. Roughly, they arranged it in the order of the Prayer Book. It was not the first, but it was certainly the first influential and successful book to print a tune with every hymn on the same page; it was also the first influential book to attach 'Amen' to every hymn—this second being a custom which editors are now gratefully abandoning.

The moving spirit—what when the project clearly was to become a large business became called the first Chairman of the Proprietors—was (savour the implications) The Reverend Sir Henry Baker, Baronet, Vicar of Monkland, Herefordshire and son of an admiral. The primary musical influence was William Henry Monk (1823–89). At the publication of the first full music edition, in 1861, these two were 40 and 38 respectively.

Among other distinctions, this hymnal is the only one about which a whole book has been written, and the story of its success can be read in *A Hundred Years of Hymns Ancient and Modern,* by

---

* AM refers to the Revised (1950) edition of *Hymns Ancient and Modern.*

W. K. Lowther-Clarke (Clowes, 1960)*. The bare bones of it are that after a trial edition was put out in 1860, the first full edition of 1861 appeared, with 273 hymns; an appendix was added in 1868 bringing the total to 386. The whole was revised in 1875 (473), a Supplement was added to that in 1889 (638). A second revision was made in 1904 (643); this was eventually abandoned and a second Supplement to the 1875 edition appeared in 1916, which was bound in with it in 1922 to form what is still known as the Standard edition, and still use in many places (779). The third full revision was made in 1950, which is still current: a Supplement, *100 Hymns for To-day* was produced to be used alongside it in 1969 but it has not yet been bound in with the parent book.

The one bibliographical point to notice is this: that essentially the 1875 edition, which means the first 473 hymns of the Standard edition, is still in use after a century. I doubt if anybody outside England can imagine just what this book meant to English people, but the quite peculiar way in which it engaged people's affections can be illustrated by a perfectly true anecdote, taken from a field of activity which is as English, and as unintelligible to anybody outside England, as the point it illustrates. It was in the summer of (I think) 1971 that, in the course of a commentary on a Test Match (those who are not English must understand that this is a game of cricket: told that, they will abandon any attempt at further enquiry), Mr Brian Johnston, one of our leading authorities on the game, announced the score in the following phrase: 'That makes it 332: that's "There is a green hill far away".'

This, I absolutely insist, so far from being a frivolous illustration, is for this subject the ideal one. Only that game produces that kind of number, and the leisure for a commentator to make that kind of remark. But only *Hymns A & M* could have been the point of reference. Nobody contradicted him by saying 'I beg your pardon: you mean 106' (or 180, or 136, or 105, or indeed 214 which would have been right for the edition of *Hymns A & M* that had been current for a good twenty years at the time of this anecdote). That is how people thought of the book: the very

---

* It may be added that the centenary was also celebrated by the appearance of the *Historical Companion to Hymns Ancient and Modern*, by Maurice Frost, Clowes, 1961, which is an indispensable work for anyone who to-day wants to study the inward history and character of the book.

numbers were sacred. It is credibly reported that by 1904, when the second revision appeared, people quite seriously complained that a book in which 'Abide with me' was no longer 27 (but became 23) was bound to be a failure: the country, such people implied, wouldn't stand for it.

More substantially we have to honour *Hymns A & M* in its early editions, of which the 1875 was the really pivotal one, for establishing for the first time widely accepted associations between texts and tunes. It was here for the first time that the tunes almost everybody now accepts for 'All glory, laud and honour', 'O God our help in ages past' (to cite it as altered by Wesley), 'The King of love', 'Abide with me', 'Eternal Father strong to save', 'Christ whose glory fills the skies', 'Hark, the glad sound', 'The strife is o'er' and 'The head that once was crowned with thorns' were set to them; and as can easily be seen, while some of these were new tunes that had immediate success, others represent marriages between partners who are well advanced in years. 'Our God, our help' (to cite it properly) was published in 1708, *St Anne* in 1708: they met in 1861.

All this can be amplified elsewhere. What interests us is the quality of the tunes that assisted the book to its success. One secret was its promotion (it hardly can be called less) of the tunes of J. B. Dykes. Dykes (1823–76) was a Doctor of Music and for most of his working life Vicar of St Oswald's, Durham; he had a remarkable gift for composing what appealed to anglican congregations—and indeed to all middle-class religious groups. As examples of the hymn-writer's art, his *Nicaea* ('Holy, Holy, Holy') and *Dominus Regit Me* ('The King of love') insist on being classed as masterpieces. The other 274 pieces in his Collected Hymn Tunes* mostly fall below this standard (the one exception is the almost unknown *Lux Vera*† which being in an unusual metre is almost unknown); but there were seven of these tunes in the 1861 edition and 57 in that of 1875. If sometimes over-consenting and over-picturesque, they are all friendly and singable, and this composer brought such hymns as 'Praise to the Holiest', 'Ride on, ride on in majesty', 'I heard the voice of Jesus say' and 'Lead,

---

J. B. Dykes: Hymn Tunes, edited by G. C. Martin, Novello: undated, shortly after 1901. The last of these (No. 276) is a setting of a hymn in Welsh.

† A & M (Standard ed.) 687.

kindly Light' into the treasured repertory of all English hymn
singers by the time his own life was ended.

Dykes's music on a larger scale was not voluminous, and certainly is not worth reviving. This special gift for miniatures was
shared by Stainer, whose *Love Divine* and *St Paul*, at any rate*
deserve to be remembered, and whose anglican chant in E minor
is a perfect musical epigram.† Exactly the same can be said of
Joseph Barnby (1838–96) whose best hymn tune *Longwood* is not
well known among anglicans,‡ and who is unfortunately more
famous for his tune to 'O perfect love'. His chant in E major is
entirely successful, and so, in a different mood, is that in A
minor.§ Even Sullivan, whose contributions to church music are
almost entirely a matter of historical interest (and, in places,
awestruck terror), managed to coin what one cannot help judging
a fine tune for 'Onward, Christian soldiers' and a very tasteful
one for 'Hushed was the evening hymn'.¶

Hymns Ancient and Modern included many trivial pieces, but
nothing like so many as Vaughan Williams said it did (see the next
chapter). Some very minor composers who wrote nothing much
else found a good length in the occasional tune, like the pious
colonel who wrote *Ewing* for 'Jerusalem the golden' (which Monk
adapted to its present rhythm) and the obstetrician Champneys
who wrote the fine chorale-like tune *St Jerome* (AM, Standard,
526), of which any eighteenth-century composer would have been
proud (and which had it borne an eighteenth-century name might
have been better known).

Of the major composers of the time, Goss contributed the entirely admirable *Praise, My Soul* (he over-reached himself in the
harmonies of verse 3 which *A & M* wisely omitted), and of course
there are the remarkably original and sometimes unsingable
tunes of S. S. Wesley himself, who, having composed them all
through his life (the earliest is dated 1830) collected them in *The*

---

* AM 205, 200.

† See *Hymn Tunes composed by J. Stainer* (Novello, 1900); especially note its modest and
generous Preface. This contains 158 pieces.

‡ *Congregational Praise*, 514 ii.

§ *Hymn Tunes by Joseph Barnby*, Novello, 1897, which is a memorial edition, using the
contents of two collections of his own completing the tally to 246 pieces.

¶ *Hymn Tunes composed by Sir Arthur Sullivan*, yet another memorial volume from Novello
(1902)—56 pieces.

European Psalmist—a fascinating hotchpotch of tunes, some exquisite, some wild—in 1872.* The indefatigable Gauntlett, who is said (one hopes unreliably) to have written 10,000 hymn tunes could on a good day produce a winner like *Irby* ('Once in royal David's city') or *St Albinus* ('Jesus lives'), and on another a carictaure like *St Barnabas* (AM Standard, 413).

All this is adduced here only as a celebration of what the hymnals did for the parishes. *Hymns A & M* was by no means the only one available. Before it there had been specialist collections like Helmore's *Hymnal Noted* (1852, 1854) and more general collections like the two editions of Chope's *Congregational Hymn and Tune Book* (1857, 1862), a very conscientious little pair which seem to be the first general hymnals (the 1857 one predating *A & M*) to insist on the 'Amen' suffix, but far from constantly as a plagal cadence in the *A & M* style. After 1861 there was a very energetic production of hymnals for anglicans, paralleled by a more sober procession of similar books for nonconformists. The Methodists revised the Wesley collection of 1780, and added a good deal to it, in 1876, there for the first time printing tunes with hymns for their people (no Amens in that book). The Congregationalists, having been content with their original hymnal of 1836 revised 1855, appendix added 1859 plus a separate tune book (the *Bristol Tune Book*) produced an orthodox hymnal of the new kind in 1887 (*Congregational Church Hymnal*); a private book by one of their ministers, the music edited by Gauntlett, appeared in 1886 as *The Congregational Psalmist*. The Baptists had *Psalms and Hymns* from 1858, and produced a music edition in 1900 calling it the *Baptist Church Hymnal*. The Presbyterian Church of England, coming late to hymnody, had *Church Praise* from 1885, but from fairly soon thereafter shared the Scottish books made nearer the headquarters of English-speaking Presbyterianism.

Nonconformity leaned heavily on the Church of England for its music; its hymnals and anthem books are mostly packed with tunes by anglican composers (and rather often hospitable to tunes which the anglican books quickly rejected); they not infrequently called in anglican editors to set the music up for them. (Gauntlett

---

* The *Oxford Hymn Book* (1908) is the best source for Wesley's tunes, but it does not contain *Hereford* (AM 329); a more accessible book, *Congregational Praise* has an unusual selection—see especially Nos. 556 and 622 ii.

above: Hopkins for the Congregationalists) only Garrett Horder's *Worship Song* (1905), that historic and extraordinary book for liberal intellectuals, which introduced to this country so much American hymnody that had never before been sung, seems to have been overseen wholly by a nonconformist editor. (Horder leaned heavily, however, on Martin Shaw's father, John Shaw, for tunes, in which, as in many other musical judgments, he was singularly unwise.)

But if there is nothing much to be said about nonconformist church music as such, except that it was exceedingly active, hearty and congregation-centred, a word must be put in here about that pervasive importation from America, the 'Gospel Song'. That is actually the American term for what we loosely call the 'Sankey' style. It is not English church music except by adoption: but when the very simple songs with fervent and visionary words and choruses appended to their tunes were introduced in the early 1870s by the evangelical missions of Ira D. Sankey and Dwight L. Moody, they proved to be so popular among people whom even the revived and strenuous orthodox churches were not reaching that they took firm root, and are very much with us still. It is a style (you find a few examples of it in the *English Hymnal*, 567–584: the section headed in very small print 'Not suitable for ordinary use') which ministers to immaturity and when over-used keeps people immature: ambulance-work (I have elsewhere called it) for people in the dreary conditions of industrial Britain but too strong in calories and short in protein to make a good diet for those who hope to grow. Certain parts of nonconformity used this style in their hymnals. *Hymns A & M* (with the single exception of 'Rescue the perishing' which had a place in 1916) would not touch it. It was, of course, a quite different approach to the problem which the High Churchmen sought to meet by reviving medieval religious pageantry in their new Gothic churches. It may be noted, however, that this kind of simple and sensational music finds a conspicuous place in the *Mirfield Mission Hymn Book* (1916, 1933), which emerged from the most notable of the post-Tractarian religious houses. Similarly, most of the hymnody of the newly-enfranchised Roman Catholics, in books from 1852 onwards, has a style very close to that of the 'Gospel songs', and was, of course, very largely provided for the popular devotion of

Benediction, at which alone, before 1964, vernacular hymnody was permitted, or for missions in those areas (the poorest areas) where the Roman Catholic faith first began to flourish after it was legalized in England.

No more need be said about all this; a modest collection of nineteenth-century hymnals, and an anthem book or two, will give the reader all the evidence he wants about the products of what was primarily an age of expansion and of practical reconstruction in all the churches. Church music was on the move, but it was suffering at this stage from wheelspin that threw up plenty of mud.

7. THE CREATIVE UNDERGROUND, 1848–1904

It is Professor Arthur Hutchings who constantly points out*
that the truth about English church music in the nineteenth century cannot be understood by looking only at England. At many
levels this is obvious, though it is sometimes ignored. For one
thing, the musical centre of Europe was at that time not in
England but in Vienna; the first half of the century is dominated
by composers of German stock, even if during the second half
more and more is heard from the French. The vocabulary of
romantic music was mediated to those middle sections of music-
making society from which the popular church music came by
way of Mendelssohn, and the elusive and uncategorizable quality
of English music during the whole century is at least made a little
more identifiable if one realizes that to a very large extent it was
the outwardness, not the inwardness—the sensation, not the intellect, of the great Viennese composers that influenced the taste
of those who created the demand.

But there is another way in which the Continent had its influence, and this was primarily through what is generally called
the Liturgical Movement. This is usually understood to embrace
the whole field in which people began to work to encourage the
people's participation in the sacred rites. The Oxford Movement
is, of course, a phase of it, but it was running concurrently in
other forms, not least musical, in Germany and France, and inspired and encouraged the promoters of the Oxford Movement,
from French clerics exiled after the French Revolution whose
presence in England sowed the seed that later came to fruit in the
re-establishment of the Roman Catholic hierarchy in England.

What this is at bottom, so far as music is concerned, is a reaction against the anti-historical mind of the eighteenth century
(and of the researchers' contemporaries in the nineteenth). We
have seen how much time the Tractarians gave to the re-
evaluation of ancient documents. The same kind of labour was
spent on the re-evaluation of ancient music. We dated the last

* For example in a somewhat temperamental but none the less informative book, *Church
Music in the Nineteenth Century* (Barrie & Jenkins, 1967).

chapter but one to 1847, and mentioned that as the date of W. H. Havergal's *Old Church Psalmody*. That is in its way a symbolic work. It is a collection of hymn tunes from such earlier sources as Havergal had access to, transcribed very inappropriately, arranged into English metres out of the more irregular ones in which they were composed, and generally giving the impression of a well-intentioned editor saying to himself rather helplessly: 'Well, I don't altogether follow this, but I suppose this is how it ought to go.' Havergal is responsible for more than one rather calamitous reduction of a beautiful original to the stature of a commonplace English tune (like the tune *Franconia*, for example), though now and again he saw the real point (as when he printed Scottish psalm tunes in their primitive rhythms).

Attempts to bring the past into the present always begin this way. The scholars grope, and back hunches, and hope for the best; only later ones peel off succeeding layers of historical accretion and satisfy the passion for exposing the true original.

A very good example of this was the Cecilian Movement, originating in Germany. Karl Proske (1774–1861) at Ratisbon Cathedral began a crusade for the recovery of the music of the Church's finest hours: of plainsong for the people, and of the Palestrina style for the choirs. Editions began to be produced, and the movement spread under two pupils of Proske. Franz Xaver Witt (1834–88) followed the Founder's principles as faithfully as he could; his younger contemporary and successor, Franz Xaver Haberl (1840–1910) yielded to the temptation to promote the composing of modern works which were deemed to be in the medieval spirit but which did little beyond putting an inhibitive religious gloss on music in a fundamentally nineteenth-century style. Cecilian Societies grew up all over Europe for the study and promotion of better church music, especially after the famous *Motu proprio* of Pius XII (1903) which seemed to call for exactly the aims the societies professed; but they got themselves a reputation for historical sentimentality rather than for scholarship or creative writing.

Users of English hymn-books will perhaps have noticed citations from the Mechlin *Gradual* of 1848, such citations normally appearing simply as 'Mechlin melody'. Mechlin is the city in Belgium later known as Malines, and as such famous in the history of the twentieth-century ecumenical movement; but the *Gradual* is the source of a few quasi-plainsong tunes which a generation ago were more popular than probably they are now. If the reader consults the two versions of *Veni Creator* at EH 154 (Mechlin on the right-hand page, authentic on the left), or those of *Pange Lingua* at 326 and 95, he will see what Mechlin stood for. Here again, the hope was that the congregation could be persuaded to take some part in the singing of the Mass and such other Offices as had by that time become congregational, and plainsong tunes were smoothed out in a cautious fashion to make them a little more congregationally accessible. Pedants nowadays throw up their hands, naturally enough, as these bowdlerized versions; but there is a strong case for saying that this, if people would get hold of it, was a good deal better than anything else they were likely to be offered in the way of modern music in 1848. Each deviation from the authentic text represents a judgment that 'they'll find this a bit easier'.

A far more venerable name, however, is that of Solesmes. Solesmes is a place in France where an abbey was founded as long ago as 1010, but after falling on bad times was re-settled by six priests, led by Dom Prosper Guéranger, in 1833 (a symbolically coincidental date), and formally reconstituted in 1837 by Pope Gregory XVI. Later in the century the anti-clerical forces in France repeatedly harassed this community, and eventually its inhabitants had to flee to England in 1901, where they settled at Quarr Abbey in the Isle of Wight until they returned in 1922. Now Solesmes threw itself into the Liturgical Movement with a much more dedicated scholarship than had been seen before, and systematically devoted itself to deciphering, interpreting, notating and performing medieval plainsong. On the whole, the standard notions of performance of plainsong current through the twentieth century take their authority from Solesmes, and the most potent interpreters of its principles to England were G. H. Palmer and J. H. Arnold (who re-edited the whole of the plainsong in the *English Hymnal* for its 1933 edition).

But Solesmes took its time, and meanwhile plenty of plainsong revival work was going on in Britain. The work of Thomas Helmore, one of our pioneers in this, has already been mentioned. He produced the *Hymnal Noted* (1852, 1854), using Neale's translations of Latin hymns and transcribing the proper plain-song tunes, and the first *Manual of Plainsong* from which congregations could sing plainsong psalms. Without doubt Helmore thought of plainsong as grave and (in the secular sense) solemn; he noted it in minims (half-notes)—and perhaps nothing did more to spread abroad the Solesmes principle that plainsong is light and flexible than Arnold's substitution for a Helmore-style in the *English Hymnal* of a new notation using quavers (eight-notes) as the standard beat.

Helmore and his friends did a power of good. But they had problems. One of these was distinguishing true plainsong from other music written down in the same kind of notation (which alone was legal in the old Catholic Church for church music). Reference has been made elsewhere to the difficulty he had in notating the tune *Divinum Mysterium* ('Of the Father's heart begotten') from *Piae Cantiones,* 1582, and his version, preserved in older editions of *Hymns Ancient and Modern,* shows, when it is compared with the version now familiar in all* hymnals, which was taken from exactly the same original, how far wide of the mark he could go.

But plainsong revival, aimed always at parish congregations, was here to stay, and the progress of those who worked at it through the second half of the nineteenth century is one of the most important gains that century can record.

Along with this can be very briefly mentioned the researches of those scholars who unearthed and imported to Britain tunes (we are still in the realm of hymns and parish music) from the Liturgical Revival of the French eighteenth century. Theses, magnificent though they turn out to be, provide a stirring contrast both to the conscious antiquarianism of Solesmes and to anything that was happening in Britain at the time. I refer here to those tunes mysteriously and somewhat coyly referred to in the *English Hymnal* as 'French Church Melodies', upon which the best authority is Fr C. E. Pocknee in his book *The French Diocesan Melodies and their Tunes* (Faith Press, 1954). Some of these are arrangements in metrical form of plainsong tunes; most are new

---

* In America only the Lutheran *Service Book and Hymnal* preserves the triple time version I refer to; elsewhere in America hymnals take the tune from an earlier plainsong source. See my book *The English Carol* (Barrie & Jenkins 1958) pp. 193 ff).

compositions of really distinguished poise and vitality. They were brought to England late in the nineteenth century by J. B. Croft, an otherwise virtually unknown priest musician, and first popularized in the *English Hymnal*. The best known is one which in English use is somewhat altered in metre, and which we use to 'O what their joy and their glory must be.' But 'O come, all ye faithful' (see above p. 48) is very much a member of this family.

Towards the end of the century the best work on plainsong was probably done by the English scholar W. H. (later Bishop) Frere, who did a great deal to spread abroad in Britain the principles of Solesmes.

All this was fortunate for English church music: if local creative talent was in short supply, we may well be grateful for the enrichment provided by foreign cultures. But if, as we trust, the nineteenth century is being rehabilitated as a period in English church music, we have not yet quite finished that story. For we must now mention the revival of carols which we also owe to these same scholars who were working on plainsong and 'Old Church Psalmody'.

Once again the hero is probably J. M. Neale so far as carols *in church* are concerned. 'Good King Wenceslas' and 'Good Christian men, rejoice' are among many of his texts that remain popular. These were occasioned by the researches of Helmore into that other aspect of medieval music—the popular songs of the time. The remarkable book, *Piae Cantiones,* published in Finland in 1582, provided a most valuable written source, and we might never have known about it had not a rare and valuable copy been brought back to Britain in 1853 by the Ambassador to those regions, and handed to Helmore and Neale (see *The English Carol,* ad loc. for some account of this.)

But this was transcribing from written sources; other researchers earlier, Davies Gilbert (1827) and William Sandys (1833) had explored the West Country of England—which remote part, as it then was, was one of the places in which the puritan suppression of these popular, legendary and imaginative songs had survived, and brought back a large collection of carols transmitted by oral tradition. As the reader can find out in the book I have just mentioned, it was not very long before (1880) the use of carols as the main ingredient in a liturgical observance began to be explored—appropriately enough, at Truro, in consequence of which carols began for the first time since the Middle Ages to find their place again in church music. The celebrated collection of H. R. Bramley and John Stainer, *Christmas Carols New and Old,* very appropriately so called because it does correspond pretty closely to *Hymns Ancient and Modern* in its field, appeared in 1871, and R. R. Chope's *Carols for Use in Church,* a more ambitious, more comprehensive and less musically reliable collection (containing carols for other seasons as well as for Christmas) in 1894. Just as with hymnody, the discovery of old carols inspired the writing of new ones. The earliest *Hymns A & M* had 82 hymns from the Latin among its first 135 (the seasonal half of the book); 48 of the 78 pieces in *Bramley and Stainer* have pre-nineteenth-century texts. It is much the same pattern.

New Blood

All this is clear gain, even if on the whole nineteenth-century editions of plainsong, carols and other older music are not now thought to be trustworthy.* It was, however, inevitable that sooner or later some serious composers would emerge who would be inspired to fill the creative gap. Just in time to be called nineteenth-century composers, they did. The first wave includes the honoured names of Hubert Parry (1848–1918), Charles Stanford (1852–1924), and Edward Elgar (1857–1934), all knighted for services to music.

There could not be a more disparate trio. Parry comes chronologically first—eight years younger than Stainer, seven than Sullivan. His opus numbers run beyond 200, and church music occupies a small space in his total output. He was indeed not a churchman but an agnostic and a subscriber to the Rationalist Press Association. But, at any rate compared with the miniaturists of the immediate past, he was a large-scale composer.

He was, however, not a cathedral composer, except in respect of a few anthems written for high ceremonials. *TECM* IV has one, 'Hear my words' (p. 158), composed for the Salisbury Diocesan

---

* Maybe not; yet I myself doubt whether anybody ever harmonized 'The first Nowell' better then Stainer.

Choral Association's Festival in 1894; this is a five-movement verse anthem, preceded by a 'symphony' and using as its fifth movement the hymn 'O praise ye the Lord', with the tune which, detached from the anthem, is now very well known. The key-relations between the movements are like those of a romantic symphony rather than those of a classic verse anthem, but its general spaciousness and treatment of the biblical text owe everything to that form. Better known, and better in every way, is the Coronation anthem, 'I was glad' (1901) with its very purposeful use of melodic themes and contrasts of key and texture, and its rousing orchestral accompaniment. The second of its four sections, the recitative incorporating the Coronation shouts 'Vivat! Vivat!' is so arranged as to be readily detachable when the anthem is used on other occasions.

Cathedral lists now quite often include pieces from the *Songs of Farewell* (1918), six unaccompanied motets which are the crown of all his choral work (one of these, 'My soul, there is a country', is the first piece in *TECM* V). Quite apart from the delicate and sensitive musicianship in every bar of these works—which range from the condensed texture of 'Never weatherbeaten sail' to the massive, almost cantata-like canvas of 'Lord, let me know mine end', these introduce another quality which this new generation of composers brought to the literature—readiness to explore the possibilities of the English poets as providers of texts. This is the best fruit of Parry's humanism. No humanist can resist the beauty of the King James Bible, whether or not he believes a word of it, but Parry's detached attitude to the church left him open to the impressions of those superb religious poets of our seventeenth century who provide texts for most of the *Songs of Farewell*; this example was followed by many of his pupils and disciples. All his mature works show a quite new sensitiveness to words, biblical or unbiblical, which we certainly see in 'I was glad' and even more in the two best of his longer works, *Blest Pair of Sirens* (1887*) and *Ode on the Nativity* (1916). Parry wrote only two cathedral services, one of which was composed before he left school (and became well known in its day), the other of which has only very recently

---

* What a year! *Blest Pair*, Stainer's *Crucifixion*, Faure's *Requiem*, the anthem quoted above and the first appearance of Sherlock Holmes!

been revived for performance. Both are in the key of D.

Parry's organ music is still played by English organists, and contains some excellent material. Its summit is undoubtedly the Bach-like prelude, 'When I survey the wondrous cross'.* He also—surprisingly for one of his attitude to the Church, wrote several hymn tunes in which he showed himself to be (as he does elsewhere) a first-rate melodist. Most of these were either commissioned or first made popular by the editors of the (1904) *Hymns Ancient and Modern.* On the borderline between hymn tune and anthem stand his exquisite setting of *Crossing the Bar* (same source) and that incomparable tune which has stood up bravely to endless hack-work, *Jerusalem.* This piece is an historic monument in the story of melody-making.

Here then was a professional through and through—capable of much dull writing, but incapable of being trivial. Stanford, who was Cambridge's Professor of Music when Parry was Oxford's, is just as professional, but a personality of different mould. Being Irish (Parry was, one supposes, remotely Welsh in ancestry but not in the least Welsh in manner), Stanford started out with a different kind of imagination, and being a churchman, he really took on the job single-handed of rehabilitating cathedral music. Like Parry, he wrote plenty of secular pieces—not in quite such great volume—and was at home in opera and symphony, even if he did not in these fields compete with the acknowledged masters. But it is always rightly said of him that he wrote his cathedral settings like symphonies (or like opera-sections), disdaining the episodic technique of his predecessors, and preferring to use real melodic development, key contrasts, and short *motifs* to bind the whole composition together. He was even more than Parry a Brahmsian (he was 19 years Brahms's junior)—as the *Magnificat* in the Service in A abundantly testifies (is this not a translation of the mood of Brahms's Second Symphony, first movement, into a cathedral setting?); perhaps only an Irishman could have conceived the unforgettable image of the young Virgin contemplating her destiny as portrayed in the solo part of the G major Magnificat; certainly

---

* I refer to the F minor prelude (detached), op. 198, not to that on *Rockingham* in the better known set.

only a musician of professional culture could have conceived the early B flat service or the late C major one. This is, in its honest way, great music and only a needlessly affected austerity will deny it that epithet.

Stanford was on the whole not a successful hymn-tune writer, although like Parry he was called on to contribute to the 1904 *Hymns A & M;* his tunes in that book (some of which died with the book) are worth studying for their unusual approach to the medium, but only *Engelberg*, for 'For all the saints' is a success—and this, by an odd quirk of history, was slapped down at once by the fantastically successful tune of Vaughan Williams and had to be rescued for a later generation by the Americans.*

Stanford even wrote one highly effective anglican chant (he wrote more, but only the A flat chant, along with the chant-setting of Psalm 150, can be called successful). On the smaller anthem-scale, his three Latin Motets (for one of which see *TECM* V p. 9), composed in 1905, correspond to Parry's *Songs of Farewell* in representing a musical profundity which elsewhere he never quite reached. He contributed some useful, if not earth-shaking, offerings to the sadly depleted organ literature of the time. And it must be said that just as Vaughan Williams constantly spoke of his admiration for his teachers, Parry and Stanford, so Dr Herbert Howells speaks also of Stanford, who was his own teacher.

Elgar can hardly go unmentioned, although he is not, in the usual sense, a church musician. His contributions to the repertory of hymn, anthem and organ are inconsiderable (apart from the Organ Sonata op. 28, which is a brave effort by a composer who is not at home with the instrument: it looks, and sounds, like an organ arrangement from an orchestral score, sonorous and inspiriting though it is). Elgar was, in the English church—himself being a Roman Catholic—an influence rather than a presence. His place in the larger story of religous choral music is assured by *Gerontius, The Kingdom* and *The Apostles*—all oratorio-scale works requiring the highest degree of skill in

---

* It is now fairly widely associated with Francis Bland Tucker's fine hymn, 'All praise to thee, for thou, O King divine'; the association was actually effected by the editors of the *Hymnal 1940* of the American Episcopal Church. It now has acquired two other excellent texts.

orchestra and singers. But to say that having music of that kind around, from an English composer who clearly established himself as the first on this scale since Purcell, did something for the *morale* of all English composers. His was an idiom which proved to 'date' rather quickly, and will probably have to wait a few years yet before its excellences are really assessed. But because he was there, others took heart.

Now what would one expect to be the next step? Why, when we turn the page and enter the twentieth century, we shall expect to find a new kind of professional approach to all that ancient music which the scholars, themselves often of limited musical talent, have been busily discovering. This, but much more, is what is waiting for our attention next. A few minor contemporaries of Parry and Stanford, whose work spans the turn of the century, remain to be mentioned. There was Basil Harwood (1859–1949), that gentle disciple of S. S. Wesley—perhaps his only one—who in a much smaller repertory showed this new sensitiveness to words; indeed, he often allowed the rhythm of the words to dictate irregular bars, which we do not find in Parry and Stanford. He was also a hymnologist, and edited that very unusual book (as indeed it ought to be), the *Oxford Hymn Book* (1908) for use in college chapels. Walter Parratt (1841–1924) was a teacher rather than a composer, but was one of the most distinguished of those who by mediating the new standards influence that new generation which was to take the centre of the stage as soon as the century had turned. We should not forget either the development of provincial choral societies, which in the second half of the century came to the height of their popularity, and had so much influence in raising people's standards of musical taste. Sir Henry Coward (1850–1944)—as a composer, rather more terrible than those we mentioned in the previous chapter—was one of the leading figures in the promotion of this sort of music-making in Leeds, and in all the great industrial centres outside London the same thing went on.

But finally—and at the risk of incurring the wrath of any reader who thinks he has had enough of hymnology—we have to mention one more jewel in the nineteenth century's crown, which is the music of Wales. This is English church music in the sense that Englishmen (as well as expatriate Welshmen) revere it, and it would be wrong to omit it altogether from this brief chronicle.

Welsh church music was until very recently hymnody first and last. It is the folk-hymnody of a people whose religion had been explosively revived by preachers associated with the eighteenth-century Evangelical Movement (principally Whitefield among the English, but many of them, of course, Welsh). People often think of Welsh hymnody as ancient and traditional. Almost all of it is from the nineteenth century—only a very few tunes from earlier Welsh ages are known (*Braint** is one, and another, we must suppose, is *St Mary*†). This is the music of a society whose churchmanship is based on the industrial village, whose people are almost all poor, and whose music is hardly at all instrument-oriented. The genius of the Welsh for singing informally in perfect harmony is legendary: the anglicizing of Wales may have gone so far now as to have nearly extinguished it. Similarly the special talent for song that seems to be bred in that race is something incomprehensible to, and occasionally envied by, the English. But what the great Welsh tunes evoke is a small, shut-in society; the chapel in the mountain-locked village, the miner's hazardous and (at that time) poverty-stricken life, and the vision beyond the ugly little utility building and the frowning slate-mined hills of the Eternal Jerusalem. Welsh religion was lyrical, fervent, biblical, and full of poetry. More mandane considerations are that, by the nineteenth century anyhow, harmony was a settled kind of music, and the major and minor scales (especially minor) the normal vocabulary. (You do not often find a modal Welsh tune unless it is very early or very late.) But when these tunes—and I refer really to those from the period 1830 to about 1890, in which period so degenerate an example as *Cwm Rhondda*, for example, does not fall—are sung by the Welsh to Welsh words, and when they are compared with what the English were producing at the same time, one hears at once the difference between a poor but homogeneous society like that of the Welsh towns and a confused and restless one like that of England. Indeed, one begins to understand a little more of what is involved in political dialogue between these two societies. For about the

---

* Songs of Praise, 505.

† EH 84, AM 309.

great Welsh tunes there is an innocent rectitude which easily yields up its secret to musical analysis: the same process which exposes the weakness of Dykes and Stainer exposes the triumphant beauty of these tunes, so many of which are anonymous, and many of which were certainly sung before they were written down. No need here for anthems, cantic settings or organ recital works. Just a fine melody and instinctive counterpoint, and you have tunes like *Trewen, Llef* and *Crugybar*, or like the better known *Hyfrydol* and *Ebenezer*. This art is actually as dead now as that of Ouseley, and Welsh music is not becoming, in the hands of such skilful composers as Alan Hoddinott and William Mathias, part of what we shall soon probably have to call British Church Music.*

---

* The best selection of 'vintage' Welsh tunes is probably to be found in *Llyfr y Tonau,* Carmarthen, 1929, the hymnal of the Welsh Calvinist Methodists: nearly all the texts are in Welsh but the tunes should interest any musician. Of English books, *Songs of Praise* (1931) and the second edition (1927) of the *Church Hymnary* were unusually generous to Welsh tunes and provide useful sources for those who cannot come by a Welsh book.

8. THE AGE OF CONFIDENCE, 1900–55

Historians of the twentieth century will be obliged to say of it that, beginning as an age of confidence, it turned into an age of rueful reappraisal. The present chapter must deal with its first half, which included both the World Wars but which stops short of the delayed-action effects of them on English culture. I am obliged to refer the reader to my book, *Twentieth Century Church Music,** which made some attempt at an assessment of the period we are about to review, and which did not go far into that which follows. Composers whom we shall mention briefly here are treated there in more detail. The relevant chapters in the books mentioned in the Preface will, of course, give further (and no doubt clearer) light on a very complicated and interesting subject.

Three streams seem to be running in this half-century: one is the stream that comes from the Parry-Stanford style; a second is that which we must associate with three composers of special importance and distinction—Vaughan Williams, Holst and Edmund Rubbra; the third is the stream of pedagogy, contributed to by distinguished musicians who turn out to be not primarily composers ᵥut communicators.

Continuing then from where we left off on the previous page, we can first say that cathedral music received a vigorous boost from the activities of several composers whose work, even during the present age of reaction, is still widely respected. These are, for our purposes (regretfully omitting others who in a larger work would get a mention) Charles Wood (1866–1926), Edward Bairstow (1874–1946), John Ireland (1879–1955), William H. Harris (1883–1973) and Herbert Howells (b. 1892).

All these have contributed music of first-class quality to the church—Harris being probably the most prolific, Ireland the least. All had some contact with the Parry-Stanford tradition at the Colleges of Music in London, and all would speak with respect of it.

The influences that in various ways were brought to bear on these composers may—having already to some extent been mentioned—be summarized thus: (1) a new interest in the sound of

---

* Barrie & Jenkins, 1964.

words, partly derived from (2) the new consciousness of the flexibility and expressiveness of plainsong, and partly from (3) a far wider knowledge than their predecessors had of the music of Continenental musicians, especially of the song-writers. We add to these (4) the new *morale* imparted to music by the great revival pioneers, which opened to English composers fields of activity that their predecessors had hardly known to exist, (5), associated with that, the new interest in music and singing imparted earlier by the great choral societies and singing schools, and now by education, and (6) a new notion of what a church musician was and what his work was about, which implied a new notion of what the Church itself was about.

If one studies the music of Charles Wood one sees a good deal of this happening at an early stage. There is about all his music a *sense of occasion,* and one realizes that this is a product of the new *morale.* Wood could write commonplace stuff (his anthem, 'O be joyful in the Lord', based on the Old Hundredth, is surely a poorish piece), but most of the time he expresses a conservative kind of confidence that must have come from his consciousness that church musicians do, after all, move in the same world as any other musicians. It is the same with Bairstow, a more committed Brahmsian than Wood, and, where Wood was a campus musician, organist of England's second cathedral, York Minster. These two composers believed that in church it was profane to be trivial, where so many earlier composers treated the church as an extension of the drawing room, and its music as a species of the *genus* after-dinner amusement. Neither Wood nor Bairstow wrote in the larger secular forms, but, in an age where in music 'secular' meant, or at least could mean, reaching the highest standards and the deepest experiences, they let secular music in, as Parry and Stanford had done. Wood's 'O thou the central orb' (set to an appalling text) I have elsewhere described as the authentic early twentieth-century cathedral sound; so, and perhaps a finer piece, is *Expectans Expectavi,* and so are several of his fine anthems founded on primitive psalm tunes. Bairstow's 'Let all mortal flesh keep silence' (*TECM* V p. 39) has an immense distance about it that makes the music a really appropriate paraphrase of the heraldic words: it is as full of mysterious atmosphere as the well-known hymn on the same text, so historically set to music by

Vaughan Williams, using a French carol tune: and one can hardly say more than that in its praise. Bairstow could occasionally write the dullest sort of *Kapellmeistermusik*,* but usually his sense of occasion was impeccable, and his ideas were commensurate with the scale of York Minster: see especially his 'Blessed city', and the supreme sensitiveness of his anthem on I Cor. 13.

John Ireland is best really as a composer of songs; his is a delicate talent that does not always stand up to the stresses of a large conception. His 'Greater love hath no man' (*TECM* V p. 57) is a late romantic masterpiece; not the least interesting thing about it is its collocation of biblical texts, which make it almost a sermon in its own right. (S. S. Westley's 'Thou wilt keep him in perfect peace' has the same quality.) But the key-relationships, the contrasting but never incongruous episodes, and the musical argument are all held together admirably, so that the climaxes have a stunning effect. His *Service in F* is perhaps less distinguished, but shows the same talent, and of course there is no better example of his feeling for words than his hymn tune *Love unknown,* now familiar to everybody, as a setting for Crossman's tender verses beginning 'My song is love unknown'; consider carefully how the high notes are placed, and the movement by step contrasted with movement by leap, the shape of the phrases and the use of free barring, and the secret is out.

Many years ago Walford Davies (of whom more in a moment) gave an example of two ways of setting the same Shakespearian text. I can do no better that cite it here; the first is by Thomas Arne, the second by Roger Quilter:

*This evocative word, which I understand not to be so much in use as it used to be, means church music written by composers who think they ought to compose but entirely

and you see what is happening to all vocal music in the time we are speaking of.

The long-lived Sir William Harris, organist at Oxford and then at St George's, Windsor, left a large quantity of church music, and it is surprising that *TECM* did not use any of it. Two pieces in OE* are good examples of his faculty, akin to Parry's but also to Ireland's, for writing a melody both strong and sensitive. These are *Vox Ultima Crucis* (45) and 'Most glorious Lord of Life' (44), both settings of classic English poems. But Harris also wrote large anthems for big choirs when the occasion demanded it. His contribution to organ literature is also substantial. He could write *Kapellmeistermusik* with the best of them (his long anthem for unaccompanied eight-part choir, 'Bless the Lord, O my Soul', 1942, is probably so classifiable), but again, here is 'sense of occasion' such as befitted an organist of a royal chapel.

Herbert Howells is a far more controversial composer than any of these—who, however surprising they were in their time, now sound demure enough. I was soundly rebuked by at least one eminent authority for writing kindly of him in *Twentieth Century Church Music,* and there are many who cannot write or speak of his work otherwise than in anger. Personally I remain unrepentant about this, but one can see why this is. More than any of those so far mentioned, Howells is an individualist in music. His music is so characteristic that you need hear only three bars of any of it to know that it is his. It always has a touch of archaistic pathos—he is steeped in the clavichord music of the sixteenth century—and often puzzles or even misleads unwary organists by writing for that instrument as if it had the clear-sounding tenor register of an early keyboard instrument. But the crown of his choral work is in *Hymnus Paradisi,* composed in the late 1930s but not performed until the 1950s, and in the series of Evening Services he has written for English cathedrals, each exploiting the architectural

---

lack the capacity to compose interestingly. It is only a description of Bairstow in such moments as 'The day draws on with golden light' (*CAB* 80: see especially the organ interlude at the bottom of p. 429 and the top of p. 430) but it is a very good description of the third and fourth rate cathedral canticle settings sometimes still appearing in their repertories. It is exactly the sort of music that the modern tendency for church music not to be composed by cathedral organists—see below, p. 112, has largely extruded from use.

* Here and henceforward, *Oxford Easy Anthem Book* (OUP, undated, middle 1950s).

suggestiveness and the special sonorities of the one to which it is
dedicated. In these he brings together the delicate song-writer's
art, in setting words sensitively, and the 'sense of occasion' which
in these cases demands gravity and high tonal colours deployed
over a large canvas. His earlier anthems, 'Like as the hart', 'O
pray for the peace of Jerusalem' and 'Mine eyes for beauty pine'
(OE 46) show the same sense of mystery and remoteness, with a
pathos that is appropriate to the kind of text he tends to choose;
this is fastidious music, more profoundly English, because more
influenced by Vaughan Williams, but with a visionary passion
which must really be traced to his Welsh forebears. A Welshman
in King's College Chapel sounds (after what we said in the last
chapter) a shade incongruous—but in a way this is what is
happening in his incomparable *Collegium Regale* canticles (*TECM*
V p. 90). No other composer, one suspects, would consider setting the *Jubilate* in E flat minor, but in that service he does (this is
not included in *TECM*).*

It is no insult to any of these composers to say that they are
towered over by Vaughan Williams and Holst: I insist on adding
to those two the name of Edmund Rubbra, a composer too little
appreciated,† whose very large output includes some symphonic
work and plenty of extra-ecclesiastical music. Indeed these three
have this in common, that they are chiefly known as composers
outside the church, but when in church they gave as good value as
they did outside it (as, we said, Sullivan, for example, did not).

Vaughan Williams is too immense to need much comment. His
church music is so well known that it comes as a surprise to learn
how small a proportion of his total output it constitutes. To get
close to him, get to know 'Lord, thou hast been our refuge' and
'O taste and see' (*TECM* V pp 23, 37). Enjoy his celebration of
plainsong, and of vulgar hymnody in the first anthem, which goes
back to 1921, and his astonishing innocence and simplicity in the
little miniature he wrote for the 1953 Coronation. Enjoy the very
characteristic humour with which, after a very long *a cappella*
passage in the first, for eight-part choir, going all over the tonal
spectrum, he brings the organ in on a foreign note which would

---

* *Twentieth Century Church Music*, pp. 55–64.

    † And, I am glad here to confess, too cavalierly dealt with in *Twentieth Century Church
Music*.

disguise any deviation from strict tonality by the singers. (That's the sort of composer who would write a concerto for tuba and one for harmonica.) Perhaps V-W towers just because with all his massive musical inventiveness he always had that touch of humanity—one need hardly be ashamed of saying, of humour. There was all the needful 'sense of occasion', as in the *Mass in G minor* or in the mysterious anthem, 'Prayer to the Father of Heaven', which he dedicated to Parry's memory in 1948.* But this same composer could always handle a 'big tune', eminently congregational and simple, as he does in the unison song 'Let us all praise famous men'.

The other very obvious thing about Vaughan Williams is that he took a view of English music that was in his early days a surprise to his contemporaries. He said that English music was not music that happened to be composed in England, but music that really derived itself from the English tradition of the greatest days, which he held to be before 1600. This simple means of putting this principle into practice was to fashion his music out of phrases that were modal rather than eighteenth-century tonal, and make his cadences match. He was a late developer, but what really set him on the course he made his own was the discovery of what could be done with modal sounds, archaic consecutives, and false relations. Perhaps he reached the height of his powers in *Sancta Civitas,* the *Benedicite* and *Job,* three of the really great religious works in twentieth-century music.

He and Gustav Holst (1874–1934) were close friends, and each believed the other quite sincerely, to be a better composer than himself. Holst was more fastidious, almost painfully self-critical, and therefore his output was far smaller. He produced very little church music because of his personal doubts about the Christian faith, which went deeper than Vaughan Williams's scepticism about the institutional church. But what he did give the Church was music that stands at the very top of its class. Sometimes he requires considerable forces and skill to do him justice—except in 'In the bleak mid winter' he was not a parish composer. His finest pieces for the church are the *Two Psalms* (86 and 148) for chorus and orchestra, the short anthem, 'Eternal Father who didst all

---

* Notice how the initial chord of this piece is the same chord which Howells uses with such telling effect at several points in the *Collegium Regale* Magnificat.

create' (*CAB* 20), the mystical piece 'The Evening Watch' for double choir and, perhaps most characteristic of all, 'This have I done for my true love', in which he brought back to Christian singers that astonishing Cornish carol which is now so well known. (The story of how alarmed the churchwardens at Thaxted were when their vicar, for whom Holst wrote the piece, posted up the text in the church has often been told: but if the carol, usually called 'My Dancing Day', is now well known, this is entirely due to Holst.) The austere simplicity of several of his hymn tunes in *Songs of Praise* makes them an ideal subject for any composer in that medium to study.

Edmund Rubbra's contribution to church music is actually larger than that of either of the others; He comes from a later musical generation (b. 1901) and the musical influences in his work are more those of the fifteenth century than of the sixteenth. These give it an elusiveness and freshness which surprises the ear that is tuned even to Holst and Vaughan Williams. He often writes in very complex textures, as in the Festival Gloria (1957) for solo voice and two eight-part choirs. The 'sense of occasion' is always present, together with great sense of distance. His *Magnificat and Nunc Dimittis* in A flat are worthy to stand beside the greatest compositions in that form, as is his *Missa Cantuariensis*. He tends to combine massive blocks of sound in fierce counterpoint, and is almost always a composer for the 'big occasion', which may be why his work is not heard as often as that of the other two; but, difficult though he often is, there is no composer of whom it is safer to say that he never wrote a second-rate passage: in that, only Holst is his equal.

Of Benjamin Britten, the next and, so far, the last of these large-scale composers, I prefer to write in the next chapter. It was another and nastier age which he served to keep sane.

Turning now to the third stream, which we can call the Teachers, we have a complementary story to tell. The first group to deal with is a group of hymnodists, and this will serve to put early twentieth-century parish customs in hymnody in their proper perspective.

At the turn of the century there were three teams at work, more or less independently, at the business of pressing parish music forward into the next stage for which, after the work of Helmore and Neale, it was ready. I refer to (a) George Ratcliffe Woodward (1848–1934) and Charles Wood, (b) Robert Bridges (1844–1930) and Harry Ellis Wooldridge (1845–1917) and (c) Percy Dearmer (1867–1936) and Vaughan Williams. In each case the first partner is a man of letters, the second a musician, and in each case they produced one or more hymnals.

Woodward, with his *Carols for Eastertide* (1894) was actually the first on the scene. He was a Tractarian priest, a member of the Cowley Fathers' Community at Oxford, and a learned and cultivated scholar in ancient hymnody. That book of carols—unusual for its date in being not devoted to Christmas—was followed by *Songs of Syon* (1904, 1910), a hymn-book dedicated to the work of reviving for English use the finest tunes of the Genevan and German past, and made possible because of his faculty for writing texts to fit the strange metres of these tunes, and the *Cowley Carol Book* (first series, 1902, second series, 1919) and the *Cambridge Carol Book* (1910). It was these two who liberated into the modern repertory 'This joyful Eastertide' and 'Shepherds in the field abiding' among many other treasures. These were strictly antiquarian enterprises. Hardly any contemporary music appears in any of them; but as a study in contemplative scholarship they are all landmarks in English church music.

The second pair, Robert Bridges (the Poet Laureate in succession to Tennyson) and the Slade Professor of Fine Art at Oxford, H. E. Wooldridge, collaborated in a similar though less ambitious enterprise—the *Yattendon Hymnal* (1899). This too was designed to rescue the great things of the past, and Bridges had the gift for writing texts of a more durable and hard-wearing quality than Woodward's, so that it was possible for quite a large part of this hymnal's contents to get into wider circulation, which, as later hymnals attest, it has done. Bridges was unashamedly pedagogic. He complained often and publicly of the triviality of parish church hymnody, and being more or less the squire of the parish of Yattendon he was able to place his Supplemental hymnal in the parish church and get it used. The full music edition of this is an enormous book, with all the tunes pedantically written out in open score, and furnished with exhaustive historical notes on each hymn.

This book was available, as Woodward's were not (except for the very earliest) when Percy Dearmer, Vicar of St Mary's, Primrose Hill, drove round in that famous cab to invite Vaughan Williams to collaborate with him in the *English Hymnal*, whose publication in 1906 represents a landmark as important as 1861 in the story of hymnody. Though the book was a very outspoken reaction against the standards of *Hymns Ancient and Modern*, the real fact is that it proposed to do for its generation exactly what the earlier book had set out to do 45 years before. But now they were in a position to say, 'This time we'll do it *right*'. It is now regarded as a 'high church' book, but it is no 'higher' (for whatever that word means) than *Hymns A & M* was in its day. The Preface makes no such claim. It simply says that the book contains the 'best hymns in the English language'—a sort of Rolls-Royce-like claim that was too broad to be seriously challenged. Certainly it showed much sterner taste concerning texts, and the standard it looked for was what it got in commissioning 'O God of earth and altar' from G. K. Chesterton. But beyond this, they now had the tools for discovering the proper versions of plain-song (Solesmes was now properly in business), and their consciences insisted that they reproduce later hymns in, as far as possible, their original versions. (This is a thing not even they could be consistent about, but they rescued many great tunes from the hideous tortures to which they had been subjected when editors tried to fit them to texts whose metres did not correspond with their own.) And—not to make too long a story of this—the same Preface contained the epic statement, which makes it the greatest hymnal preface since that of John Wesley, that 'good taste is a moral concern.'

Those were Vaughan Williams's words; his senior partner, Dearmer, was a crusader as much for the abandonment of sentimentality in liturgy as for its extrusion from music. 'Let's do it *right*' meant, among other things, 'let's be real historians, not romantic ones'. Just as Vaughan Williams wanted, not nineteenth-century approximations to old texts, but the old tests unvarnished, so did Dearmer think about liturgy; for his a sham Gothic church with cheap and shoddy fittings was much worse than an honest nonconformist chapel. Beauty, he held, could never be got at cut rate; it must be paid for, not only in money, but in what money properly represents—the honourable labour of taking trouble. This was the content of the new wave of high-church aesthetic.

This naturally brings us to a quartet of teaching musicians—who since two were brothers almost count as a trio: Sir Walford Davies (1869–1941), the two Shaws, Martin (1875–1958) and Geoffrey (1879–1943) and Sir Sydney Nicholson (1875–1947). And a very mixed bunch they are.

Walford Davies, organist of the Temple Church in London and then, just before Harris, of St George's, Windsor, was a musician who took the high tradition of church music from the cathedral into the parish, and indeed into the schools. Of Welsh nonconformist ancestry, he always had a peculiar and personal feeling for the sheer beauty of sound. As a composer of miniatures (where like the Victorians he was at his best) he employed free rhythms and shapely melodies to express the sound of words: his very well known 'God be in my head' is an epitome of his style, with its warm sound, its rhythmic flexibility, and its choral enrichments at the end (a device he rarely left unused). But Davies became nationally famous for two things especially: the promotion of speech-rhythm chanting in psalms—thus rescuing the anglican chant from the 'parish thump' that had brought it into disrepute, and for being the first musician to use broadcasting as a teaching medium. His life was wholly spent in the church, and he came out of church to spread enthusiasm for the beauty of music among as wide an audience as he could find. In his broadcasts (in which he showed himself a master of the medium) he would be as likely to talk about a Chopin nocturne or a Schubert sonata-movement as about church music, but his aim was to bring them together.

The Shaws were of a different stamp. Geoffrey, the younger, spent his working life in schools, ending as an Inspector. Martin spent his youth in a series of almost bohemian adventures, including conducting for Isadora Duncan, and though he became most famous as an advocate of good church music the theatre was always in his soul, and his best compositions are songs in the manner we just now associated with his younger contemporary Ireland. Geoffrey was patient and industrious: Martin, explosive and articulate. Both of them spent much time in the parishes, but

Martin had more time to give to it, and he also had an especially, passionate concern for English music that put an edge on the advocacy of Vaughan Williams. Martin went so far as to say that all English music before 1914 was German music (as least, since Gibbons), and he put it that way because of the impact of World War I. As a composer he is best known for the Folk Mass, Merbecke's only serious competitor in the days before the liturgical reconstructions in the Church of England. He became Percy Dearmer's organist and devoted friend, and with him helped to edit (the final music arbiter being Vaughan Williams) the two editions of *Songs of Praise* (1925, 1931) and the *Oxford Book of Carols* (1928). Those two books were the best things done during that period towards the disseminating of good musical taste among the parishes and among the young: *Songs of Praise* found its way into many State Schools (better received there than in the churches) and the carol book has remained the carol equivalent of the *English Hymnal*—the book nobody can ignore. The name of the two Shaws appears constantly in both, more as arrangers than as composers; but it was these two who really visited the country churches and talked to people whose affections had to be weaned away from the drearier aspects of Victorian anglicanism.* If Walford Davies took great church music to the people, Martin Shaw was quite as much an apostle of great secular music and its standards as the message the Church needed to learn. He, rather than Walford Davies, would speak of the intolerable 'churchiness' of most people's customs, and urge on them the folk music of the remote past, or such church music as sounded strange in their ears, in order to widen their vocabulary and elevate their taste.

Sir Sydney Nicholson was different again. The Shaws and Davies came from humble backgrounds; Sydney's father was a neo-aristocrat who had been one of the founding fathers, and the first Chancellor, of the University of Sydney in Australia (hence his name, Sydney being born when his father, who lived to be 95, was 67 years old). Nicholson was a cathedral organist—going into the music profession very much against the wishes of his parents, who were of the culture that still thought music a ragged and unworthy calling: a cathedral organist to them might just about be

* See, if you wish, my short book, *Martin Shaw, a Century Appreciation* (Martin Shaw Trust, 32 Museum Street, Ipswich), 1975.

on a level with a decent butler. He became organist of Carlisle Cathedral, and later of Westminster Abbey, but he resigned from the Abbey to found the School of English Church Music in 1927, making use for this purpose of his social connections and his ample personal fortune. Thus he harnessed the special advantages of his birth to a purpose which without them could hardly have been achieved. The institution he founded is now, of course, the Royal School of Church Music and the leading teaching institution in that field in Britain.

The dignity of Walford Davies, the bustling energy of the Shaws, the calculating business enterprise of Nicholson—taken together these qualities in musicians, all of whom subdued what composing talents they may have had to the more important purpose of teaching and communicating, proved to be the forces which built up the English church music tradition to the level which it achieved by 1940. It was really possible to say by then that the things these archetypal teachers had said against every possible prejudice and discouragement in the early days were taken largely for granted. You never heard bad chanting in a cathedral by the middle of the century; you noticed a real raising of the standards of parish hymnody; even when they were using old hymnals their choices were more careful. Schools were teaching children the things Shaw and Dearmer had introduced to them, and increasingly integrating music into their regular curricula. Vocabularies at every level, from the cathedral choir through the post-1944 School Assembly to the country parish in Lincolnshire were being widened. Everybody now knew Vaughan Williams's tune to 'For all the saints'.

The nonconformists were also undergoing a certain musical reconstruction. You might say that a sort of nonconformist Oxford Movement took place in the late 1930s. Not that it was a concerted movement as was that of the Tractarians; but theology of a new-orthodox kind was bringing all the major denominations to re-evaluate their customs of worship, and especially to elevate the Communion services from a level of pious domesticity to something more like a ceremonious Eucharist. Organizations like the Church Order Group, among Congregationalists, the Methodist Sacramental Fellowship, and comparable movements of less organized opinion among Baptists, not to mention the Iona Community in Scotland which affected the whole Presbyterian communion in Britain, were all saying, so far as worship went, rather Dearmer-like things. Music began to take the hint. The Congregationalists produced in Eric Thiman (1900–75) their own brand of Martin Shaw, and the Methodists produced similarly Francis Westbrook (1903–75). These in their generation advocated higher standards, less casual approaches, more professional attitudes, among people who were far less biddable than the anglicans among whom the Shaws worked. As composers they set a decent example without in the end making the grade of greatness—but it was a shining example compared with what their people had been used to. As teachers and influences (Westbrook was a minister as well as a D.Mus, Thiman a lifelong professor at the Royal Academy of Music) they were pioneers. Nonconformist church music does not call for the same range of productiveness that the cathedral tradition generates; but a fairly steady stream of workmanlike anthems began to appear from nonconformist composers, chiefly Thiman, in a style which owed a good deal to that of Martin Shaw—melodious, candid, not particularly original; not showing much sign of internal growth but at least avoiding the sensational idiom to which their congregations had grown accustomed in previous generations. They moved slowly enough to be able to take their people with them, and that in its day was perhaps the best service they could offer.

The ecumenical movement was, in Archbishop Temple's words, 'the great new fact of our time'; that is, the great new fact of the early twentieth century. In church music it meant that the ordinary people of different Christian communions began to hear each other's music. Music had, of course, never confined itself within denominational frontiers, and hymns and anthems within the various traditions tended to spill over into others through the work of editors and publishers. But a new consciousness among nonconformists, whose musical ethos tended to be hearty and activist, of the possibilities of the more professional and contemplative approach of the cathedral style, created a modest demand in some churches for a new approach to music-making, and subtly changed the repertory. Non-anglican choirs began to appear in robes (unheard of in the nineteenth century); undigested bits of anglican liturgy crept into nonconformist services, not always with any kind of appropriateness. Bad editions of the Tallis responses appeared in the backs of hymn-books, and you might even hear an anthem in Latin now and again. This, one might say, was a fairly negative kind of ecumenicity, and it was not until a little later that one could say that the different music-making streams really took one another seriously.

But since the ecumenical movement among the people in the pews was much less the effect of high-level conversations between bishops and moderators than of nonconformist boys and girls going to anglican public schools, Baptist girls marrying anglican boys, Methodist trippers calling in at cathedral evensongs in the summer, and Congregationalist children of musical promise being sent to get a good education at cathedral choir schools, one would expect the effects to be somewhat accidental and unorganized. One has also to say that the tendency, after the days of conflict when nonconformists went to prison rather than pay rates to support anglican schools (which did happen around 1902), for nonconformist churches to be built with chancels and transepts, and for the never wholly absent feeling that the anglicans really knew how to do things properly to come to the top, had much to do with the so-called 'improvement of taste' in nonconformity. In this period the great anglican teachers, the Shaws and Nicholson, had no knowledge of the existence of any church but the Church of England (Walford Davies, we must admit, did, and wrote music for at least two Congregationalist publications), but none the less non-anglican choirmasters were overhearing what they had to say. In hymnody, the effect of the *English Hymnal* on *Congregational Praise* (1951) was, to take one example, the consequence of the social and accidental kind of ecumenicity rather than of the imminent foundation of the British Council of Churches. Joint worship on large occasions between all Christians (before 1964 these would not include Catholics) in a neighbourhood, promoted by ecumenical organizations, did nothing interesting for church music; more unstructured contacts did far more.*

---

* Non-anglican choirs were first allowed to be fully affiliated to the Royal School of Church Music in July 1968. Non-anglicans had been instructing in its short courses at least since 1949.

One might expect, as has just been hinted, that the ecumenical movement might have its most evident effects in hymnody, the most mobile of church music forms. Again, in the early part of the century this is less positive than it later became. Two non-denominational hymnals *Songs of Praise* (enlarged, 1931) and *The BBC Hymn Book* (1951) show some signs of being thus influenced. *Songs of Praise* was most at home in non-denominational worship such as its chief promoter, Percy Dearmer, was by that time offering at the Guildhouse in London, or in schools, especially after the Education Act of 1944 which enjoined non-denominational daily worship on all state schools; and its contents were 'ecumenical' in another sense because of Dearmer's special admiration for the nineteenth-century liberal American hymnody which began by being a Congregationalist preserve in England. *The BBC Hymn Book* was a real attempt, by anglican editors who were on the whole ill served by the Dissenting authorities whom they asked to advise them, to provide an ecumenical book that would serve for the daily broadcast service.

But this movement needed time to get itself really working at parish level, just as the Oxford Movement had needed it; so in the period 1900–50 we find the anglican style of church music developing steadily and confidently and building on the constructive practical work of the previous century, and nonconformist music enthusiastically but uneasily assimilating what its promoters could use. Anglican vicars were learning fairly well not to treat non-anglican ministers as people who might spit on the floor, but the time had not yet come for nonconformity to develop a non-imitative attitude to church music. What one has a right to expect, of course, and what we may get yet if we are patient enough, is the injection into the stream of musical thinking of that spirit of critical and creative theology in which nonconformity really did excel in its best days. It is not very cheering to have to say that just when it has a chance of being a creative force, the one skill in which nonconformity really used to be professional seems to be evaporating.

9 ANXIETY AND OPPORTUNITY, 1955–75

In gentler days it was always regarded as decent to end any historical book about twenty-five years before the time of writing. History now moves so quickly that there is no need to do any such thing. The only restriction it seems proper to observe is to refrain from offering critical judgments about one's contemporaries and juniors—but it becomes, at this point, necessary to evaluate what is being done by people who are achieving distinction in the field we are working in. And as everybody knows, after 1955 church music in England suddenly began to receive a number of violent shocks from people who began asking fundamental questions of a sort that before this had never been raised in the circle of musicians.

It all goes back to a crisis in people's thinking about the Church and about the Faith itself. On the whole, the area in which church music in England has flourished most freely—that of the cathedral service—has not been the arena of theological discussion, still less the arena of lay thinking about the role of the Church. It is perfectly proper—it is an enormous blessing—that there should have been an area of security within which church music could develop itself, an Establishment which made the world reasonably safe for it. The more secure that area, the freer the musicians were to pursue their orderly and decorous course. Few even among radicals would really wish King's College, Cambridge, to abandon its style of music-making and conduct itself like a suburban Presbyterian church.

But one does see a quite new style of choral music appearing in the field of church music, which has been generated by a new and strictly contemporary demand. I refer to this at once because if I am permitted in any sense to be hortatory, I wish to be so here. I mean the demand created by the sudden establishment in England and Scotland of new university campuses, so that by 1965 or so England had, instead of Oxford and Cambridge and a few respectable nineteenth-century provincial universities, as many universities as it has dioceses. A quick look through the productions of such able composers as John Gardner, John Joubert and their contemporaries indicates a fairly steady stream of commissions from campuses for anthem-style pieces to celebrate special occasions in their youthful histories. Now some of the new campuses are wholly secular and disdain even campus chapels. Others have buldings of a fairly traditional style: yet others have chapels in styles which are in the best sense experimental (such as the University of Sussex)—and here, of course, we have at last stumbled into using the word that dominates all theological and liturgical thinking in the present age. But such chapels, and surely all campuses, have singers: choirs of young and teachable people, male and female, who are happiest with music that has a more 'open air' sound than that of the traditional cathedral style. A famous example of music so commissioned is Joubert's *The Holy Mountain,* a short anthem for choir and two pianos. Where would you ever find two pianos in a cathedral? But it is more likely that you will find them than a cathedral organ in a modern campus assembly-hall. If asked to produce one choral piece which wholly reflects and then transfigures the 'experimental' spirit of the youthful 1960s, that is the piece I should unhesitatingly choose.

Now if it is true that cathedral choir schools are threatened by economic pressures and government policy on education, and cathedral authorities are in a state of anxiety about the future of their music, two things can be said. One is that (as I shall say in a moment) cathedrals are finding new ways of discharging their ministry in which music takes and will continue to take a leading part; the other is that the campuses should be encouraged to take and to expand their responsibility for causing the composition of good religious music. This should not end with their foundation Commencement-exercises. They can be—without massive inroads on their budgets even if they behave properly—valuable patrons of music that seeks, as the cathedral music at its best always did, excellence and distinction.

We begin at that point so as to establish the atmosphere of 'the experimental' at the beginning of this chapter. But nobody will assume that cathedral music is yet showing signs of extinction. The rule we enunciated near the beginning of this book still holds: creativeness is not greatly discouraged by adversity; but (another point we are about to make emphatically) it can be corrupted by misdirected enthusiasm.

Returning, to our main theme of 'new thinking about the

church': what is a campus community centred on chapel or religious meeting house but a new kind of religious community—a community like a school in changing almost all its personnel every few years, but unlike a school in being voluntary, and composed of more mature people? It could not be less like the old-style college chapel in Oxford or Cambridge. It is composed of people from all religious backgrounds or none, articulate, chattering, strenuous and often rebellious. 'Obedience' is not their most conspicuous quality, nor is 'routine' (or 'daily Office') their favourite activity. They are asking always, 'What's new?' and the church musician's answer can take its cue from St Paul who was among university people in Athens who were constantly asking that (Acts 17.21). He said, in effect, 'What I am offering is newer than you can imagine, but maybe you will have to come back here to see it.'

But one can hardly expect the twentieth-century citizen to have St Paul's poise or patience. What, in fact, was new in our century? Five things are new, or, if old, hailed as new.

(1) The revolution in thought concerning the axioms of music, that had prevailed since Bach and evolved without serious disturbance, were questioned by people who, before about 1950, had no noticeable effect on church music. The revolution is commonly traced back to Debussy and Schoenberg, who were born respectively ten years before and two years after Vaughan Williams. Perhaps the first appearance of what could be called a 'twelve tone' touch (it is no more) is in the *Sanctus* of Britten's *Missa Brevis* (1960), and the first short anthem to make use in any sense of this style may have been Frederick Rimmer's 'Sing we Merrily' (1963). But in both these the serious 'twelve tone' style is incorporated as an ornament rather than as a principle.

Mention of that distinguished Scottish composer gives us the occasion to remark that it is only in our century after a lapse of more than four hundred years, that a substantial Scottish contribution is being made to church music. The Scots rely less now on immigrant English musicians, and if it is too early, as it clearly is, to claim that a Scottish style is appearing, the very remarkable contribution of Scottish composers to the *Church Hymnary* (Third Edition, 1973) indicates a new self-consciousness in that nation which, if it is at present operating mostly on an academic level, holds out plenty of hope.

Church music has naturally been cautious of atonality and aleatoric music, but modern composers for the church have not been unaware of what has been developing in the whole relation between composer and listener in the concert hall. Some modern theories of worship, which question the whole basis of 'participation' on which traditional worship rests, are bound to generate all sorts of new and suggestive musical forms, and in America there is a good deal more experimental in both areas than at present the mainline anglican tradition finds room for. But even in Britain, organists who play Messiaen cannot be deaf to what he, a profoundly committed Christian, has been saying for forty years now about the forms of church music.

The very existence of Michael Tippett's *Magnificat* and *Nunc Dimittis* (1961)* indicates a healthy awareness of the possibilities of a sort of music which even twenty years before would have been regarded as impracticable in the English church.

(2) Equally important is the new kind of judgment made about the secular and its relation with the sacred. This is familiar in theological conversation as being associated with the 'South Bank' theology of the mid-sixties, but it is something much wider than that. For various reasons the dividing line between what is thought of as secular and what is judged sacred has been totally obliterated. Musically this in itself is healthy. It means the removal of a superstition. Neither Purcell nor Bach made the slightest distinction between sacred and secular music: all respectable composers have distinguished only between music that is, and music that is not, applied to sacred uses. But the hectic speed with which judgments were made in the sixties obliterated another distinction which we cannot do without: that between the secular considered as excellent and the secular considered as vulgar.

In the music of Benjamin Britten for the Church—and he has made a handsome and distinguished contribution to the literature all the way from *A Boy was Born,* op. 3, to the *War Requiem* op. 66, via such delights as *Rejoice in the Lamb* and the *Missa Brevis,* not to mention his series of church operas—we see

* The *Nunc Dimittis* is at *TECM* V p. 143.

an illustration of 'the secular as excellent', or 'the secular as un-
distorted.' The same talent that goes to *Billy Budd* goes to the *Cantata Misericordium; Midsummer Night's Dream* is made of the same
stuff as the *Festival Te Deum*. Compare that with Sullivan, or even
with Mendelssohn (where did he offer the Church anything so
exquisite as *his* Midsummer Night's Dream?) and the non-
pejorative sense of 'secular' corresponding with the best
theological impulses of J. A. T. Robinson, Leslie Newbigin and
Daniel Jenkins, is at once illuminated.

(3) But turn from Britten and his disciples to the self-styled
Twentieth Century Church Light Music Group, whose compositions first appeared in 1956 (the late Geoffrey Beaumont,
1905–71, being the Group's chief advocate), and another
meaning of 'secular' seems to be implied. One thinks of Britten
saying in one tone of voice, 'let church music be less inhibited',
and one hears the Light Music composers saying it in another.

This becomes a little clearer if we mention the widespread
questioning of accepted axioms about church custom and
behaviour which accompanied and in the end probably generated
much of the popular church music of to-day. If we pick up that
word 'inhibition', which we used a moment ago, and ask what it
is that the reformers want set free, we are bound to hear that
some want music set free to be music, while others want people
set free to do as they like. It really is not unfair to say of most of
the so-called 'Light' music, which never claimed to be great
music, that it does not chime with that aspect of the Church which
says 'No' to Satan; those who promote it are over-anxious to
represent the Church as saying 'Yes' to everything, and the
assumption that the Church can never be right if it is in dispute
with the secular world is one that, in logic, let alone theology,
nobody has the right to make.

But the insistence that the Church offer hospitality to life-styles
which it dismissed too casually in the past has plenty of sup-
porters, and rightly so. The setting of old hymns to jaunty and
musically slovenly tunes is one thing: the writing of new songs for
the Church to sing, with appropriate music, is another. Sydney
Carter (b. 1915) is the central figure in this phase of church music,
and even if he constantly says that he does not write church
music, he is much sought after in some forms of Christian

worship, and he certainly has every right to be thought of as a Christian prophet. With a modest but decisive talent in music, and a facility with lyric that at least once, in the song *Friday Morning,* showed prophetic theological genius, Carter stung the conscience and enlarged the compassions of a whole generation.

But look how he did it. He can, as he admits, compose only melodies: others must harmonize them. They are mostly solos, or ballads with choruses. He sings them in a voice which is deliberately untrained, and sets them in keys which no cathedral trebles could possibly reach. He disputes and renounces the 'bel canto' style of singing, and approves the hoarse and withdrawn techniques of the pop-singers. So when he produces one more rasping ballad about the hypocritical triviality of orthodox Christianity, he disseminates a singing technique that goes with it, almost leading us to assume that 'bel canto' and Christian complacency are inseparable.

(4) The questioning of axioms about how things are done in church, our fourth concern, is a phase of this. Bascially a function of the youthful rebellion against all the axioms of a world that produced Auschwitz—for it is in the sixties that the real effects of the two World Wars made themselves really inescapable—the 'pop culture' is sternly and puritanically moral; indeed, it is always puritanically intolerant. And therefore it has to be said that all the very proper and often creative suggestions that are now made about the supplementing of the organ with other instruments in church, or the de-professionalizing of church music, or the usefulness of 'folk' hymnody have always been embittered by this hasty and intolerant moralism, so that in the church all these movements have become divisive. Sydney Carter becomes the patron saint of the new philistinism, which is the last thing he wanted to be.* Malcolm Stewart, a more sensitive and orthodox folk-composer, is still undervalued† because he gives nobody a chance to distort his work into bitterness.

(5) But in the end, it is the slower and more measured rhythm of change that finds sympathetic vibrations in the Church at large. The folk, the vulgar, and the informal, all of which have their

---

* See Sydney Carter's *Green Print for Song* (Stainer & Bell, 1973).

† See *Gospel Songs for To-day* (Geoffrey Chapman, 1971).

value, are still eccentricities; people still think of them as 'experimental'. But all over the English scene (and elsewhere) liturgies have been revised, Bibles retranslated, and worship-customs reconstructed. The effect of this on musicians has sometimes been discouraging. The promoters of the nineteenth-century Liturgical Movement and of the Oxford Movement would be delighted to see the modern tendency, in all the churches, towards the reinstatement of the Eucharist as the Church's central act of worship. The Parish and People Movement in the Church of England was the direct outcome of 1833. But parish musicians find themselves being asked to abandon those approximations to the cathedral tradition which had given them the best chance of making music at the level they most valued. As for the composers, they have wrestled with the new liturgies, and usually lost. It is hardly unsafe to say that there are now dozens of settings of the Anglican 'Series III' available; it is, however, fair to say both that the language of these liturgies is not necessarily so discouraging to artistic setting as the first wave of conservative protest claimed, and also that the real difficulty has been found to be to find settings that avoid both vulgarity and too much complexity. The abandonment of Merbecke has been as traumatic in the parishes as the abandonment of Latin has been to many Catholics. Things would have gone better had a few musicians been in close and intimate touch with the development of the new liturgies, instead of being relegated, when they were used at all, to a rather remote 'consultant' or 'correspondent' status.

So much happened to the English Church in the third quarter of the twentieth century that it is not surprising that the main outward quality of that period must be restlessness and confusion. The startling consequences of the Roman Catholic Vatican Council have induced a quite new relation between Roman Catholics and other Christian bodies, and have made it legitimate for members of that Communion not only to talk freely to others and join in ecumenical activities, but to ask, and not necessarily to be satisfied with the traditional answers to, every kind of theological and moral question. Naturally the liturgical reforms within that Church have called for a considerable new output of Catholic music since 1964, perhaps the most active strain of which is in hymnody, for which a sudden new demand has made itself felt. It must be said that the work of English editors and composers has, until very recently, proved to be a good deal more level-headed than that of their cousins in America.* The Irish composer Michael Dawney (b. 1944) and the American Noel Goemanne are showing what fine music the new dispensation may produce if the congregations give it its chance.

But despite all this there is still a discernible 'main stream'. *TECM* V has, in its second half, some very good examples of the new kinds of music. It does not feature John Joubert, whose music ever since his first well-known piece, 'O Lord the Maker of all thing' (1945) has shown a consistently alert and professional approach to the new styles. But John Gardner (p. 163) in 'O clap your hands' (1953), his op. 15, shows an early promise of liveliness which his later output has fulfilled. Peter Maxwell-Davies (b. 1934: see p. 196) has a remoter, more contemplative idiom which uses sounds that reach right back to Taverner, while they are, in his hands, sounds which only a mid-twentieth-century composer could make. Geoffrey Bush (b. 1920, p. 173) in *O Salutaris* gives us what may be one of the most beautiful miniatures of his generation, and makes us wish that there was more church music where that came from. Kenneth Leighton (b. 1926), English born but professionally associated through most of his working life with the university of Edinburgh, shows himself in 'Give me the wings of faith' (p. 180) a craftsman of great imagination: even more so in his now well-known *Crucifixus pro nobis* (1961). Along with these there are Anthony Milner (b. 1925). Tony Hewitt-Jones (b. 1926), Bryan Kelly (b. 1934), William Matthias (b. 1934), Peter Aston (b. 1938) and John McCabe (b. 1939), all of whom are musicians who move freely in the secular world, and give of their best whichever mode they are writing in.

Indeed, what is really surprising is that we can name only two contemporary cathedral organists who are composing vigorously for the Church—Francis Jackson of York (b. 1917) and Arthur Wills of Ely (b. 1926). This, when one compares the state of things

* The hymnals *Praise the Lord* (1972) and *The New Catholic Hymnal* (1971) both contain material of a quite new and characteristic kind; in the U.S.A. the 'popular movement' has produced a very large quantity of trivial, mediocre, and 'disposable' music, reaction against which is really to be found, so far, only in *Worship II* (1975), most of the valuable new music in which is not by Catholic composers.

a hundred years ago, when church music was being written so largely by people who wrote only church music, is a dramatic change. It would be too much to claim that the disappearance of creative talent from the organ loft is an unmixed blessing, but it is certainly true that church music has been freshened and cheered by the insights of people who habitually move in a larger field. The very small, but very distinguished, contribution of Sir William Walton to church music is a good example of what we here mean. It could not be less (in the boring sense) 'churchy' yet not a note of it is incongruous or ill-judged.

You can say that an age that could produce Britten's *Missa Brevis* (1960: see *TECM* V p. 156) is not an age to be desperate about; and I myself should say that developments since the deadline date of my book *Twentieth Century Church Music* (which was 1962) have in thirteen years tended to show that church music, in a time of deep ecclesiastical soul-searching, has begun to find a new *morale*. In the realm of hymnody, which in the early sixties looked like being engulfed in the swamp of pseudo-popular trendiness, the new freedom seems to be welcoming certain gentle disciplines, with results that can easily be found in the best of the new Supplemental hymnals. Indeed, in the very existence of a whole series of Supplements one detects a timely wisdom in their promoters; it seems to have been agreed that this is no time to be sure what great material in the older sources should be discarded, but that it is a time when so much new insight is being gained that new material must be put in the hands of congregations; Supplements, that keep the parent books alive but add new treasures, are the obvious answer, and every major denomination now has one.* Perhaps it is a shade disappointing that nonconformity as such is as yet producing nothing on a larger scale than some useful new hymns; but then we have to concede, what we mentioned at the beginning of this chapter, that in the Church of England, apart from a clamorous demand for settings of the new liturgies, the cathedral repertory as such is not expanding particularly vigorously, and the parishes are not at the moment looking very hard for new choral works. The constituen-

---

* Anglican—*100 Hymns for To-day* (1969) and *English Praise* (1976); Methodist—*Hymns and Songs* (1969); Baptist—*Praise for To-day* (1974); United Reformed Church (formerly Presbyterians and Congregationalists in England)— *New Church Praise* (1975).

cy that makes the most useful demands on composers is, or should be, that new kind of Christian worshipping community that forms itself in the new social milieux of modern England: primarily, as we said, the campus.

To draw all this together, and to resist the temptation to go in detail into what historians will certainly later judge to be the most fascinating period in all English church music, I draw attention to three forces which seem to typify the English scene at the point where we leave it. One is a cathedral, one a teaching institution, and one a composer.

The cathedral is that of Coventry, which since its re-opening in 1962 has proved to be a centre of modern liturgy in an entirely unusual sense. Coventry is where within weeks of the rededication ballet-dancers were exercising their art in a Cathedral Festival (and people wrote to the papers about that); it is where the late Duke Ellington made one of his last and most memorable appearances. It is where Britten's War Requiem was first sung. A collection of its service-papers for special occasions is, for any who can assemble it, the finest source for practical liturgical construction that could be asked for. In any new service, whether it be the Dedication itself or the public memorial of some distinguished citizen, scholarship, poetry and a high sense of occasion combine to produce that which is natural, beautiful and simple: dignity and wit, friendliness and a sense of great occasion, combine here in the choice alike of words and music to provide what the most sensitive mind must respect, what must nourish the most sceptical.

Yet in the booklet which a member of the congregation receives at Evensong, the 'daily office' (musically celebrated there only at the week-end) there is this memorable passage, which I quote here by kind permission of the Cathedral authorities:

When you come to Evensong here, it is as if you were dropping in on a conversation already in progress—a conversation between God and men which began long before you were born, and will go on long after you are dead. So do not be surprised, or disturbed, if there are some things in the conversation which you do not at once understand.

Evensong is drawn almost entirely from the Bible. Its primary purpose is to proclaim the wonderful works of God in history and in the life and death and resurrection of Jesus Christ. Its secondary purpose is to evoke from the worshipper a response of praise, penitence, prayer and obedience.*

I quote also this, the Collect, composed by the Precentor for the service at the beginning of 1973 to remember and offer the perplexities and hopes of Britain on the founding of the European Economic Community:

Come, Father and Lord, creator of this beautiful
    and hospitable world,
Come, Lord Jesus Christ, the light which the darkness
    has never mastered, and never will,
Come, Holy Spirit, Lord and life-giver,
Come, Lord, come:
Accept the tribute which we pay
    of gratitude for the graces and beauties of Europe
    of sorrow for the follies and cries of Europe,
    of reverence for the sanctities of Europe:

Come, puissant Lord,
    refresh us with the riches of thy creation,
Come, benign Redeemer,
    rescue us from the misuse of thy creation,
Come, Holy Spirit, the only Ruler of our unruly appetites
and   affections,
    dispose us to share the resources of thy creation,
Come, Lord, come:

Create among the nations of Europe
    justice
    and comity,
    and joy;
    for now all things sigh to be renewed,
    and only in thy will is our peace;
    who reignest God,
    today,
    tomorrow
    always.
        AMEN.

---

* *Evensong in Coventry Cathedral:* (p. 13) obtainable from the Cathedral Office, Coventry.

That is an atmosphere in which the high tradition of English church music can thrive: an atmosphere of benign authority and cheerful obedience. Who can charge antiquarianism or (damnable word) irrelevance against that? Who can accuse it of treadiness and triviality? Any who wish to study twentieth-century liturgy, the true nursery of great church music, must attend to the Coventry liturgies.

Secondly, and in a sense arising out of that, we should mention the development of the Royal School of Church Music. This institution is serving its founder's purposes in ways he never dreamed of, but ways he would mostly have rejoiced in. It serves them in three ways: by promoting the highest standards of teaching for church musicians, by keeping alive a network of communication with the parishes through its Commissioners, and by sponsoring large festivals of church music usually in diocesan cathedrals.

It is these last which are the most spectacular products of its work. Hospitable now to Christians of all denominations, the RSCM encourages the gathering of diocesan choirs in one place, whenever it is possible, to make the kind of music that so many parishes, either because of their slender resources or because of new liturgical policies, cannot make. This again keeps alive the music-making tradition and irrigates with a festive refreshment the routine of parish music. It also gives the cathedrals something new and important to do, and re-establishes them as 'Places of Learning and Influence in the Community'.* Cathedrals ought to be that in ways other than musical, but there is no doubt at all that college, cathedral and parish are most fruitfully brought together in these festivals. All we wish is that perhaps a little more commissioning of new music for such occasions could be undertaken.

But if there is one musician who seems to be becoming the central figure, or at least who may well be judged so in later ages, in the church music of the third quarter of our century, it must be Malcolm Williamson, who was born in 1931 and appointed

---

* That phrase is taken from the title of Albert van den Heuvel's two lectures, *Cathedrals as Places* &c, given at Coventry Cathedral in 1966 and obtainable from the Cathedral Office: the second of these especially is a statement with which any who are in charge of cathedrals or large churches, especially city churches, should be familiar.

Master of the Queen's Musick in 1975.*

We place him thus precisely because of his elusiveness and his
refusal to be categorized. Here is, you might say, the diametric
opposite of Rubbra and Howells. He writes, and has written, in
many styles so different that hardly any other composer can be
thought of who has attempted such diversity. He came into the
English consciousness first as a composer of hymns in an alar-
mingly offhand style, which were admitted to the charmed circle
of the Light Music Group (about 1960); but he soon appeared as
a composer also of serious organ music, of operas, and of
demanding choral pieces. His music is by turns lyrical and severe.
The composer of *Phoenix at Coventry* has often been heard to say
how much he admires the talent of Joseph Barnby. And the composer of *Julius Caesar Jones* has given his talents more lately to the
composition of miniature church operas, performable by
children with the congregation joining in here and there, like
Genesis and *Winter Star*. By turns he can shock and charm, and
more than anyone else he can come right down from Olympus
and mix with the children of the market-place. He owes a good
deal to Vaughan Williams's sense of humour and to Britten's
magic with sounds. Consider the varieties of style, the blending of
hearty earthiness with mystery, of almost harsh sounds with
seductive sounds, in his short cantata *Harvest Thanksgiving,* and it
will be obvious that future historians will have more difficulty in
placing him than they will have with any other composer. They
will be irritated by this untidiness: but if they want to call it confusion, plenty of others will want to call it compassion—and
there, in a couple of words, you have all the exasperating and
endearing contradictions of the late twentieth century.

There we must leave it. Whether the English tradition in church
music will continue as a separate tradition may perhaps be
doubted. *TECM* V contains one piece by a Scot, one by a Cana-
dian and one by an American composer, suggesting that the lines
of nationalism even here are less easy to draw than they used to
be. But to the extent that the English church remains English, a
tradition will continue, change how it may. And the heart of
it—this must be gratefully admitted by a non-anglican writer—is

* This is the first time since the office was inaugurated in the reign of King Charles II
that a Master has been as much as forty years younger than his predecessor

the music of the Church of England; its uniqueness corresponds to the uniqueness of the Church of England. Nowhere else (not even elsewhere in Britain) is a protestant Episcopal Church in the majority; so nowhere else is there a cathedral tradition of music such as prevails in England. Nowhere else has a liturgy as light and hospitable as that of Evensong been available to nourish church music in the high style.

If, however, music-making among English Christians depended solely on the cathedral tradition, the outlook might be sombre. It is to be hoped that it will never be extinguished: but if it were, others would be making music, or the music made in cathedrals would take a different form. What would be a disaster is the possibility of the tradition's being buried under a wave of populism. Not all decisions can be rightly taken by popular acclamation; not all precious heritages are built up on majority votes or by committees. According to the demand, so will music be produced. Attempt to restrain it, and it will still flourish as it has done in critical periods in the past. Demand transitory, disposable, instant-sensation music, and it will be provided. Insist on that, and the high tradition can easily be buried. It is not restraint, but demand that determines the quality of a church's music. The signs now are favourable; nobody need assume as of right that they will remain so.

De capo

By way of postscript, let me advise any reader who has persevered thus far to return to the Preface, and consider enlarging his information by referring to some of the books mentioned there. In particular, any who wish to turn their attention to practical matters in Church music should possess Lionel Dakers's book, *Church Music at the Cross Roads*, where he will find not only much valuable material in the body of the book, but some indispensable guides to repertory in the Appendices, and a most illuminating article, right at the end, by Alan Gibbs on the repertory in contemporary music.

Many excellent composers have been crowded out of this short work, and samples of the work of some of them, in all periods, can be found in the anthem collections we have mentioned. But a great deal of good twentieth-century choral music is not in collected editions, and has to be obtained in octavo form. Those who are interested in building up a collection of such material for themselves may be glad of the following advice: the first step is to obtain current catalogues from publishers, to see what remains in print of the work of any composers you are interested in. Your choices can then be ordered direct from the publishers, or preferably through the Publications Department of the Royal School of Church Music (Addington Palace, Croydon, Surrey CR9 5AD) who are skilful at handling these matters. The College can also give valuable information about recordings of church music and can usually handle orders for them.

The pursuit of church music is an enjoyable business.

INDEX

Alta Trinita Beata, 12
Amner, J., 23
Anglican chant, 39, 43, 52
Arne, T., 91
Arnold, J. H., 80
Arnold, S., 41
Aston, P., 111
Attwood, T., 41, 43
Augustine, St, 5

BBC Hymn Book, 103
Bach, J. S., 19, 10 *et al.*
Bairstow, E., 89, 90, 91, 92n
Baker, H. W., 70
Barnby, J., 73, 116
Bastwick, W., 25
Batten, A., 23. 29
Battishill, J., 41, 42
Beaumont, G., 108
Beggar's Opera, 44
Binney, T., 52
Bishop, J., 38
Blow, J., 33
Book of Common Prayer, 26, 38, 57, 70
Book of Homilies, 20
Boston, N., 54
Bourgeois, L., 17
Bridges, R., 96
Brighton, 59
Britten, B., 49 *et al.*
Bull, J., 23
Bush, G., 111
Byrd, W., 21 *et al.*

Calvin, J., 15
Camden Society, 62
Campuses, university, 104, 105
Carols, 12 *et al.*
Carr's Lane Church, Birmingham, 52
Carter, S., 109
Carver, R., 8
Cathedrals to-day, 115
Cecilian Movements, 78
Champneys, R., 73
Chapel Royal, 7, 8, 22, 23
Charles II, King, 30, 32, 37, 116n
Chesterton, G. K., 97
Child, W., 33, 37

Chope, R. R., 74, 82
Clark, T., 54
Clarke, J., 35
Conditor Alme Siderum, 4
Cooke, B., 41
Cornyshe, W., 8
Cosin, J., 25, 38n
Costa, M., 65
Coward, H., 86
Coventry Cathedral, 113, 114
Croft, J. B., 81
Croft, W., 36
Cromwell, O., 25
Crotch, W., 41, 43
Curwen, J., 52
Curwen, J. S., 52

Dakers, L., 117
Daman's Psalter, 19
Damett, T., 7
Davies, H. Walford, 91 *et al.*
Dawney, M., 111
Day's Psalter, 19, 23
Dearmer, P., 96
Dearnley, C., 28, 35
Debussy, C., 28, 106
Denmark tune, 46
Dowland, J., 19
Druitt, R., 62
Dunstable, J., 7, 8, 9
Dykes, J. B., 72, 73, 88

Ecumenical Movement, 101
Edward VI, King, 14
Elgar, E., 82 *et al.*
Elizabeth I, Queen, 14, 20
English Hymnal, 97
Epiphaniam Domini Canamus, 6
Este's Psalter, 19
Eton Choir Book, 12
Evensong, 58, 113, 117
Excetre, J., 7

Farmer, J., 19
Fayrfax, R., 8
Fellowes, E. H., 22, 50, 67
Foster, M. B., 68, 70
Frere, W. H., 81

Frost, M., 71n
Frye, W., 8

Gardner, J., 104, 111
Gauntlett, H. J., 52, 74
Gelineau, J., 6
Genevan Psalters, 17
Gibbons, O., 23 *et al.*
Gibbs, A., 117
Gilbert, D., 81
Giles, N., 23
Goemanne, N., 111
Goodwin, T., 18
'Gospel Song', 75
Goss, J., 66, 73
Greene, M., 36
Gregory XVI, Pope, 79
Gueranger, P., 79

Haberl, F. X., 78
Hackett, M., 62
Handel, G. F., 36 *et al.*
Harris, W. H., 89, 92
Harrison, F. L., 6n
Harwood, B., 86
Havergal, W. H., 78
Hayes, W., 36
Helmore, F., 62
Helmore, T., 62, 79, 80, 95
Henry VIII, King, 13, 15
Heuvel, A. van den, 115n
Hewitt-Jones, T., 111
Hill, R., 52
Hilton, J., 23, 26
Holst, G., 89, 93, 94, 95
Hook, W., 61
Hope, A., 62
Hopkins, E. J., 18, 75
Horder, W. G., 75
Horsley, W., 54
Howells, H., 89, 92, 94n
Huddersfield Choral Society, 65
Hullah, J. P., 62
Humfrey, P., 33
Hus, J., 15
Hutchings, A., 37, 77
Hymns Ancient and Modern, 73 *et al.*
Hymns, nonconformist, 74
Hymns, Roman Catholic, 75
Hymns, Supplemental books of, 112

Hymns, Victorian, 70

Injunctions, 20, 25
Ireland, J., 89, 91, 98

Jackson, F., 111
Jenkins, D. T., 108
John XXII, Pope, 5
Johnston, B., 71
Joubert, J., 105, 111

Keble, J., 55
Kelly, B., 111
Kirbye, G., 19
Knox, R. A., 16

Lacey, T. A., 13
Lampe, J. F., 44
Langton, S., 9
Laud, Abp W., 24
Laudi Spirituali, 12
Lawes, H., 33
Le Huray, P., 19, 27n, 28
Leighton, K., 111
Leo I, Pope, 5
Lock Hospital, 44, 52
Locke, M., 33
Long, K., 41
Lowther-Clarke, W. K., 71
Luther, M., 14, 15, 16, 17

McCabe, J., 111
Madan, M., 45
Magdalen Hospital, 45
Manning, B. L., 1–2
Mary, Queen, 14
Mathias, W., 111
Maunder, J. H., 65
Maxwell-Davies, P., 111
Mechlin *Gradual*, 78
Mendelssohn-Bartholdy, F., 77 *et al.*
Merbecke, J., 26, 27, 99, 110
Messiaen, O., 107
Methodism, 54
Milner, Anthony, 111
Milton, J., 33
Mirfield Mission Hymn Book, 75
Monk, W. H., 70
Moody, D. L., 75
Morley, T., 19, 23

Mundy, W., 23
Murray, G., 6n

National Society, 61
Neale, J. M., 62 *et al.*
Newbigin, L., 108
Newman, J. H., 55
Nicholson, S. H., 98, 99
Nonconformity, 74 *et al.*
Novello & Co., 66
Novello, V., 53

Office Hymns, 11
Old Hall Manuscript, 12
Oliver, 7
Organum, 4
Ouseley, F. A. G., 62 *et al.*
Oxford Bach Choir, 65
Oxford Movement, ch. V, 64, 77, 100, 103, 110

Palmer, G. H., 79
Pange Lingua, 3, 79
Parish and People Movement, 110
Parker, M., 19
Parratt, W., 86
Parry, C. H. H.. 82 *et al.*
Passion Chorale, 4ɕ
Pepusch, J., 44
Pius XII, Pope, 78
Plainsong revival, 80
Pocknee, C. E., 80
'Pop culture', 109
Porter, W., 29
Power, L., 7
Proske, R., 78
Prynne, W., 25
Psalters, metrical, 16, 19
Purcell, D., 35
Purcell, H., 34, 86, 107
Puritanism, 14 *et al.*

Queldryk, 7
Quilter, R., 91

Rainbow, B., 62n
Ravenscroft, T., 19
Reese, G., 4n
Reformation, 5 *et al.*
Restoration, 23 *et al.*

Rimmer, F., 106
Robinson, J. A. T., 108
Rogers, B., 36
Royal School of Church Music, 100, 102n, 115
Rubbra, E., 89 *et al.*

St Barnabas, Pimlico, 63
St Bartholomew's, Brighton, 59
St Mark's, Chelsea, 61
St Michael's, Tenbury, 62
Sandys, G., 81
Sandys, W., 33
Sankey, I. D., 75
Schoenberg, A., 28, 106
Schools, music in, 100
Scotland, music in modern, 106
Sequences, 11
Series III, 110
Shaw, G., 42f, 62
Shaw, J., 75
Shaw, M., 62, 75, 98
Simper, C., 65
Smart, G., 61
Smart, H., 70
Solesmes, Abbey of, 3, 6, 79, 80, 81, 97
Songs of Praise, 99, 103
Spohr, L., 65
Stainer, J., 65 *et al.*
Stanford, C. V., 82 *et al.*
Steggall, C., 70
Sternhold, T., 17, 18, 23
Stevens, D., 6
Stewart, M., 109
Sullivan, A., 65 *et al.*
Sumer is icumen in, 6
Sumner, W. L., 61
Sussex, University of, 105

Tallis, T., 21 *et al.*
Tallis's Canon, 48, 49, 53
Tate and Brady, 38
Taverner, J., 6, 8, 9, 10, 111
Temple, Abp, W., 101
Thiman, E. H., 101
Tippett, M., 107
Tomkins, T., 23, 26
Travers, J., 36
Turle, J., 54

Twentieth Century Church Light Music Group, 108

Vatican Council II, 1964, 110
Vaughan Williams, R., 65 *et al.*
Veni creator Spiritus, 8, 9, 25n
Veni sancte Spiritus, 8, 9n
Victimae Paschali, 3
Voluntary (Organ), 10

Wales, music in, 87–8
Walmisley, T. A., 61, 66
Walton, W., 112
Watts, I., 38, 44
Webb, B., 62
Weelkes, T., 23
Weldon, J., 36
Wood, C., 89. 90, 96
Woodward, G. R., 96
Wooldridge, H. E., 96